Praying New Beginnings

Mining Old Testament Law for
Daily Leadership Guidance

John P. Chandler

Illustrated by Jessica Luttrull

Foreword by Alan Hirsch and Mike Breen

Genesis-Deuteronomy

Copyright © 2013 by John P. Chandler.

Published by **Uptick Imprint,** 4 Lee Court, Lake Monticello, Virginia, 22963, USA.

All Scripture quotations are taken from The New Oxford Annotated Bible containing the Old and New Testaments, edited by Bruce M. Metzger and Roland E. Murphy, New Revised Standard Version, Oxford University Press, New York, NY, 1991, 1994.

Design: Jessica Luttrull
USA ISBN-13: 978-0-9890816-5-8
Printed in the United States of America. First printing, 2013.

Get the free "Praying the Old Testament" app!
Go to www.SpenceNetwork.org/Praying on your Safari site.

Library of Congress Cataloguing-in-Publication Data
John Chandler, 1961-

Praying New Beginnings: Mining Old Testament Law for Daily Leadership Guidance

ISBN-13: 978-0-9890816-5-8
1. Leadership; 2. Discipleship; 3. Old Testament; 4. Devotionals

What others are saying about the "Praying ..." Series

"John's gift of helping leaders look at their role through the lenses of scripture is a gift that is beyond measure. This book is a sacred offering to those who have been called and entrusted to lead. Seasoned leaders and emerging leaders will be inspired to lead others in "the way" that will provide the most significant imprint a leader can leave – the imprint of Christ."

Jan Bazow
Founder and CEO, Fortis Group | Richmond, Virginia

"Some pontificate on leadership without actually getting their hands dirty leading. Some leverage leadership ideals to boost their ego rather than to lay down their life for God's Kingdom. It's rare to find someone who surrenders themselves to the tiresome work of leading with both humility and courage. Even rarer is when this person can also guide us along the same path. John Chandler is one of these rare leaders."

Winn Collier
Author, *Holy Curiosity* | Pastor, All Souls Charlottesville | Charlottesville, Virginia

"John Chandler is the kind of guy I from which I want to learn about Scripture. He knows and loves the Bible. He understands our world. He studies leadership (and leads well himself). And he cares about

people. Working through the reflections, I've seen first-hand how John's combination of scholarship and experience makes "Praying" simple but not simplistic, scholarly but not pedantic, and inspirational but not sappy."

Travis Collins
Author, *Tough Calls* | Pastor, Bon Air Baptist Church | Richmond, Virginia

"John Chandler is a follower of Jesus who will captivate you as he takes you on a personal journey through God's word. He will challenge your thinking and call you to act on the same verses that led to the God stories we all love! As someone who has had the privilege of being before Kings, there is no experience greater than being in the presence of the King of Kings. John is a personal friend and a leader who demonstrates Christ-like love. I know he will inspire you as he has me, to live out God's word."

Jimmie Davidson
PEACE Pastor, Saddleback Church, California | Founding Pastor of Highlands Fellowship, Abingdon, Virginia

"There is no compromise for principle-based leadership and John's **"Praying"** books are extraordinarily inspiring. These books give each of us insight which can be applied not only to our roles as leaders, but also importantly, who we are as followers. John is truly one of our most prized thought leaders and I am left inspired following every interaction I have with him. These are books I will keep at my side and recommend to all who humbly strive to lead and follow as God would have us do."

Tiffany Franks
President of Averett University | Danville, Virginia

"Working with college students, I know the importance of quick and memorable coffee house communication. Jessica Luttrull has an artist's knack for communicating complex concepts in ways that are catchy, memorable, and even profound. Pair that with John Chandler's concise discoveries of biblical wisdom and you get an elegant, potent, and useful daily handbook for growing as a biblical leader."

Evan Hansen

Director of Eunoia | www.beautifulthinking.org | Charlottesville, Virginia

"John Chandler has shaped countless ministers through his tireless commitment leadership development. I am blessed to be one of them. As a leader of leaders, many of whom have no formal biblical training, I am grateful for this leadership development tool. John has made biblical wisdom accessible, impactful and memorable for Christians at all levels of leadership and all stages of spiritual maturity. Visual learners like me will love the drawings that anyone can replicate as they share these nuggets of wisdom with others."

Wendy McCaig

Author, *From the Sanctuary to the Streets* | Founder and Executive Director, Embrace Richmond | Richmond, Virginia

"I have been studying the Bible now for over six decades, and I am continually amazed at the fresh insights God provides me each time I open His book. In his **"Praying"** books, my good friend John Chandler also provides some fresh, practical insights into how to make your Bible study more productive and how to become a better leader in the process.

Focusing on the Old Testament, particularly its leaders, John reviews a chapter, highlights a truth and then makes a practical application.

Read this book because it's witty, insightful, and practical, but also read this book because it is written by a proven leader who knows what he is talking about, who has dealt with the enormous challenges of training young ministers to be more effective in advancing the kingdom in a culture that, morally, looks very similar to Israel over 3000 years ago.

John's leadership of Spence Network has transformed the lives of many young ministers and better prepared them to take on the challenges of leading the church in the 21st Century. I have seen the result of John's work first hand in the transformed lives of many young leaders he has invested in; his book may transform your life as well."

Bob Russell

Author, *When God Builds a Church* | Bob Russell Ministries | Louisville, Kentucky

"The power of the Baptist movement in history is its belief that any person has access to the heart of God through Jesus Christ. When we humbly submit ourselves to the Bible and see ourselves reflected there, we can trust that the Holy Spirit will speak to us, and that we can hear, respond, and lead. This is one reason I am excited that my friend and fellow leader John Chandler has written these leadership devotionals. These reflections are both suitable for presidents, and for ordinary folk on church nominating committees. They will help anyone who wants to lead biblically and lead well. It is my hope that every Baptist in Virginia and around the world who has to make decisions will use John's book to turn *their hearts to the God of the Bible who can give wisdom for daily leading. Trust me, you will be changed and you will be a better leader!"*

John Upton
Executive Director, Baptist General Association of Virginia | President, Baptist World Alliance | Richmond and Falls Church, Virginia

"Great Bible exegesis is only truly great when it spans the millennia to inform and inspire our world today. John Chandler has that unique ability to interpret scripture with integrity and application. Moreover John's own walk with Jesus matches the words he brings to print. I thoroughly commend John's writings to anyone looking to strengthen their walk with Jesus.

Craig Vernall
National Leader, Baptist Churches of New Zealand | Tauranga, New Zealand

*"John Chandler has provided a key ingredient in the formation of any effective congregational leader: regular, consistent, insightful and inspiring study of scripture. His insights are simple, yet profound. His approach is extremely user-friendly and accessible. His knowledge of congregational life is not naïve or divorced from reality. I am grateful for this powerful addition to our efforts to raise up leaders for God's people in the 21*st *century."*

Bill Wilson
President, Center for Congregational Health | Winston-Salem, North Carolina

Dedication

To my grandparents: Lonnie Preston Sprinkle and Eva Kate Stevenson Sprinkle, and John Edward Chandler, Jr., and Edith Ometa Watson Chandler:

Thank you for being people of the Book, and for quietly teaching me by demonstration both to love it and to try to live it.

Thank you for the Genesis of each of your lives, and for the new beginnings you made possible for me and for many.

"What you once believed, you now see!"

Table of Contents

Foreword to the "Praying" series

By Alan Hirsch and Mike Breen

Those who would reactivate the missional church must first awaken a missional form of discipleship. Clearly, it will take the whole people of God – apostles, prophets, evangelists, pastors, and teachers – to catalyze a movement of the Kingdom of God in the West. We are long past the day of believing that this movement can rest alone in the hands of superstar preachers and celebrity Christians. Every revolution is led by an uprising of peasants, not the edict of kings. And the revolution of Jesus' Kingdom breaking in on earth as it is in heaven is no different. It will take place when ordinary disciples lead the church in the world.

But where are all of these ordinary apostles, prophets, evangelists, shepherds, and teachers going to come from? From disciples who are becoming more acculturated to the ways of Jesus than tamed by pervasive cultural mores. And they are going to become acculturated to Jesus' forgotten ways by learning a rhythm of daily engagement with his presence.

The early church exploded from a minor sect to a world movement when it embraced an "all-hands-on-deck" missional form of living and leading – that is, when *every* follower of Jesus did the heavy lifting. Ordinary people had to act as apostles, prophets, evangelists, shepherds, and teachers. No one sat on their hands and waited for the twelve famous people who walked with Jesus to do all of the leading. And if we want to see the West today transformed from dying Christendom to a reawakened missional movement of the Kingdom of God, then it will take all of us being better leaders.

The only way we become better leaders is by becoming better followers, better listeners. We are all going to have to embrace a spirituality that learns to listen to and follow the God of the Bible.

If you want to sit around at Sunday lunch and argue that if your preacher would only preach a little better, then all would be well, you are sadly mistaken. Sure, better preaching is helpful. But alone, your pastor is not enough, and preaching is clearly not enough. It will barely budge the church, let alone the neighborhood – or the world, for heaven's sake! It doesn't all depend on platform people. It depends on all of us being disciples, and on disciples being leaders.

This is why I am so excited about John Chandler's series of books that demonstrate a path for praying through the Bible. Even better, these are excellent, mature, articulate, and distinctly *adult* types of reflection. There is a scholarly depth and social breadth beneath the concise and understandable applications of Scripture. But though academically and theologically sound (and at times profound), what we come out with when we read these reflections is *clarity*. Things are clear enough that I can scribble them down on a napkin and show you something that might inform a decision you have to make that day. We learn to listen to the Bible with the full expectation that God will speak to us. And as God speaks to us and leads us, we become more capable of leading others as well.

The "*Praying*" books have credibility because they already have had impact on groups of young adult leaders that John leads called "*Uptick*." It is part of the training: they learn from John how to engage with the Bible and catch the rhythm of discipleship, learn to live dynamically engaging God's Kingdom in the world. This in turn has been part of reshaping his tribe, Virginia Baptists, into one of the most refreshing and innovative denominations I have experienced in the last few years. As James Davison Hunter has written, movements that "change the world" start through activating small, tight networks. Jesus himself said that the Kingdom of heaven is like a mustard seed. Amazing things happen when ordinary leaders live as listening disciples.

I know that John has shared this kind of teaching with some of the most powerful and influential leaders in the world. But what I really like is that this kind of "octane" is available to ordinary disciples. This is not just a book for pastors; this is a book for *you and me.* If you will begin to catch the rhythm of listening to the God of the Bible by following John's lead, you will become a better disciple and a better leader."

Alan Hirsch
Author | Activist | Dreamer
The Permanent Revolution, Untamed, The Forgotten Ways, The Shaping of Things to Come

Here's the thing: Without a proper rhythm of life, it is impossible to hear the voice of God and experience the leading of the Holy Spirit. Going "OUT" to the world or "IN" to your close relationships without the "UP" of daily listening to God lapses into empty activism or self-indulgence. Until we learn to abide and await direction from the Word of God in Scripture, we are, in Paul's words, little more than "*noisy gongs or clanging cymbals*" (1 Corinthians 13:1).

In saying this, I could not be more pleased that my friend John Chandler has written this "***Praying***" series through the Old Testament. Understand from the outset, this isn't an attempt to cover every chapter of the Old Testament. He is not trying to offer the final, definitive picture of what God says there. Far from it. He is instead inviting you to *join him* in his practice of listening to God, participating in the "UPward" relationship of abiding, resting, pausing, waiting, and listening – which usually precedes a word from God. **If you learn to do that in these selected chapters, you will learn to do so in many other chapters not covered here.**

Take the example of learning to ride a bicycle. Maybe you were taught to ride by a parent, sibling or friend who walked beside you as you started unsteadily. Walking alongside you slowly at first, then guiding until you gained momentum and confidence, they then let you go. The steering became easier as you learned to pedal more rapidly. And once you learned to ride a bike, you never forgot. This is what John is trying to do in these reflections. He is modeling the way, walking alongside of you, helping you gain speed – and he will let you go in order to explore on your own the rest of the Bible in all of its riches.

At least in my understanding, this is one of the most biblical ways of teaching. Jesus drew his disciples around him so they could learn by watching. Paul repeatedly said to his churches, "*Imitate me as I imitate Christ*" (1 Corinthians 11:1, Philippians 3:17, 2 Thessalonians 3:7, Hebrews 13:7, etc.). John himself has a track record of offering his life and leadership to other disciples so that they can learn to grow in the rhythms of Jesus. And in this book, he is offering a way of imitation to you. We never get to innovation by mere information; it takes imitation as well. And if you will learn to imitate John's practice of listening daily to the Bible and expecting God to guide you, you will grow as a disciple of Jesus.

Maybe we can use a quick example.

Many of us have probably had someone in our church community approach us with a measure of frustration and say, "Can you help me read this book? No matter how much I try, I can't seem to understand what I read in the Bible. It doesn't always make sense." What do most of us do? Well, we probably give them a book that was particularly helpful for us; maybe we ask some questions; but we probably also show them *how we engage with the scriptures!* That's what we are talking about here. There's information we give, but then we flesh it out with a real-life example. We realize that the purpose of imitation is that it will lead to innovation.

I am particularly excited for the visual material accompanying these reflections. Don't let the simple nature of the sketches fool you. Their power is found not only in how they capture the big idea of the reflection. The drawings are powerful because they enable you to understand and pass along that big idea to another person. Again, true discipleship is not merely listening "UP" to God or taking information "IN" to your own heart. Until we pass along the word of God out to others, we have not "closed the circuit." And these illustrations will help you lead "OUT" by giving you a concrete way of sharing what you have heard. *It makes it reproducible!*

In my own experience, having visual material (LifeShapes) is a way of helping people who learn by sight and by touch in a different way than conceptual learners. Art makes material available to a whole different group of people, and perhaps to a whole different sector of your heart. These sketches are catchy, memorable, and portable. They can be cross-cultural and cross-generational. The artist, Jessica Luttrull, has done us a favor. She has made her work repeatable. By offering art that we can sketch to others, she has created a vehicle for us to grow in being disciples and making disciples.

In short, I hope you will not only read the book, but learn to imitate the way that is modeled here: to listen expectantly, discern clearly, and lead biblically. John is an apostolic leader, and I am seeing evidences of "torches" he is lighting with young leaders ("Uptick") and other Virginia Baptists who are imitating him as he imitates Christ. They are growing and paying it forward by teaching others to be disciples of Jesus. We want to see these torches become "bonfires," missional centers not only in Virginia, but around the world. I pray that as this book helps you set your rhythm of life with Jesus, your life will become a torch that will become a part of this larger bonfire.

Mike Breen
Global Leader, 3D Ministries | Pawleys Island, South Carolina
Author, *Building a Discipling Culture, Covenant and Kingdom*

Preface: *How this book began*

I experienced the great blessing of growing up in a time and place where reading the Bible was intrinsically valued as the path to personal transformation. If you wanted to know and grow with the God of Jesus Christ, then the first and best way to do that was to study the Bible.

My grandfather would quietly mention that he read entirely through a different translation of the Bible every year. My blind grandmother would listen to recorded cassette tapes of scripture and often memorize entire chapters at a time. In my Sunday School at Friendly Avenue Baptist Church in Greensboro, North Carolina, we turned in weekly offering envelopes with checkmark answers to the personal question, "Bible Read Daily?" Once I became a teenage disciple of Jesus Christ, I learned to read at bed time my "Good News" version of the Bible, with its simple but interesting stick-figure illustrations.

Bible study which began as an adolescent conviction then developed into adult academic pursuit at the university and seminary, and later a vocational habit as a pastor and teacher. I have since experimented with creative ways to continue engaging with the Bible diligently, such as listening to spoken scripture while riding my motorcycle. Leviticus is never as interesting as when blared at eighty miles an hour!

Several years, ago, my friend Mike Breen challenged me about the discipline of "winning the first battle of the day" – that is, to engage in listening conversation with God through the Bible before turning to the inbox and my work for that day. I decided to do away with my first-thing-in-the morning habit of two newspapers and ESPN

SportsCenter, and devote myself instead to serious, daily reflection on one chapter of Scripture every day. With strong coffee and my cat Mingo at my side, I began to consolidate lessons and sermons from a quarter-century's worth of previous teaching alongside of new study, and to record the key notes in the margins of a single preaching Bible. What I initially feared would be an hour or two I couldn't spare every day became the best practice I undertook, as I became a calmer, clearer, more effective leader. As my personal muscle for the practice developed, so did my ability to lead others to do likewise.

A relational network is a powerful thing, and through one such network, I met a very important leader, one whose daily decisions impact untold numbers of people. The short version of the story is that my wife, Mary, and I began to pray daily for him. And I began to email this leader two to four brief reflections every week from the Old Testament as I studied every day. I tried to hone in on leadership insights and how a chapter might give guidance for daily decisions such leaders face. Whenever God impressed something upon me through daily study, I captured it in a brief email, and sent it forward.

I found this idea of leadership guidance to be a fascinating lens through which to engage with the Bible. I also found that whatever guidance I sent to this leader was often useful to share with others. Often I would diagram on the back of a napkin a simple picture to capture the core daily insight. Over time, as I tried to lead, teach, and mentor, this became a habit. After a year's worth of doing so, Mary suggested that I compile these reflections into a book.

There are 187 chapters in the Old Testament Torah, and I have written 169 reflections, occasionally combining more than one chapter into a single reflection when the line of thought made sense to do so. The Torah or Law is about "new beginnings" – the beginning of the earth, the start of leaving slavery and living as free people, the initiation into an orderly way of life, the launch of life as the people of God in the Promised Land. *Praying New Beginnings* is an effort to unpack the successes and failures of the people of God to capitalize on these new beginnings. As we learn from them, we have an opportunity to leverage their stories for the benefit of our own. Creation is an ongoing process, and we can re-create well when we listen well to our first stories of creation. In Genesis through Deuteronomy, there are many demonstrations of what makes for good and bad leadership. What I share here only scratches the surface. I believe that anyone who will engage in disciplined listening to the material in the Law will find many more (and better) insights about leadership than are captured here!

While I want these specific devotions to guide leaders in daily decisions, I hope even more deeply that they model the way to form habits or "build the muscles" of disciples to listen every day to God through scripture. When leaders are habitually disciplined to engage with the Bible about their leadership, they will be amazed at the guidance that comes from God. It is *"new every morning"* (Lamentations 3:23). I am certainly finding this to be true, as the verse with which my grandfather charged me at ordination to ministry is unfolding in my life:

> *"The Lord God has given me the tongue of a teacher, that I may know how to sustain the weary with a word. Morning by morning he wakens – wakens my ear to listen as those who are taught." – Isaiah 50:4*

I pray this work will help to waken your ear as you lead.

John P. Chandler   9

Introduction: *Goals, Audience, Methods*

Goals

The premise for this book is a simple one: reading the Bible expectantly can change your life as a leader. If you will discipline yourself to come to Scripture every day with the conviction that God will offer concrete guidance for your life and leadership, you won't be disappointed. There will be "fresh bread" given to you as surely as God gave Israel manna in the desert. And, when you learn to capture these biblical insights in simple pictures and pass them "on the back of a napkin" to other leaders, you will unlock great power for yourself and for many.

My goal is to model the way for you to do this so that you can build the muscle to make it the time signature in your rhythm of life.

Mike Breen teaches brilliantly of the imagery of the work of finding wisdom. Citing Job 28, he says that our job is to "dig" or "excavate" the precious gold of wisdom under the surface. Sometimes wisdom simply comes to us through an <u>eruption</u> of the Holy Spirit, like lava from beneath the earth's surface spouting from a volcano. Other times, we gain wisdom the hard way – through <u>erosion</u>, where suffering strips away the topsoil of our life, revealing precious but hard-won metals underneath. But beyond eruption and erosion is a third way: the way of <u>excavation</u>. Here, we dig a shaft beneath the surface soil until we find the gold underneath.

Here's a picture:

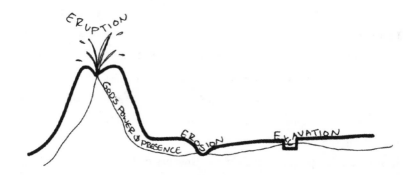

This book is not only a collection of nuggets I have mined and want to pass along, but is written in hopes that you will learn to be a miner, too. If you read and treat this simply as a collection of someone else's devotional thoughts and stop there, then I will have failed in what I hope to achieve. There's plenty more gold "down there." And my goal is to model the way until you learn to dig for yourself! (You know, teach a person to fish and ....) Again, I believe that if you excavate Scripture expectantly and with discipline, you will never be without the guidance of the Holy Spirit in very concrete ways that inform your life and leadership.

Audience

This book is for leaders. Before you opt out and say, "I'm not a leader" – if you have formal or informal influence over another person, group, or situation, you are indeed a leader. And you can benefit from turning to the Bible with an eye for what it has to say about leadership. I hope pastors and Bible teachers will be able to use this book, but even more, it is for managers, school teachers, bank tellers, students, CEOs and landscapers.

We look at the Old Testament Torah or Law because this portion of Scripture contains our first stories of "new beginnings."

They contain many case studies of the great good that can be done through effective leadership (even in dark times), as well as the great harm done by squandered leadership opportunities. They hold a treasure trove for listening leaders who are willing to excavate in order to learn on the dime of others. Our first biblical leaders were great listeners to God. My conviction is that, for Christians, leadership should be viewed through the lens of discipleship. The best leaders of people are the best listeners or followers of the God of the Bible. The core work of leading is to listen to our Leader before we try to lead anyone else anywhere else. We build the muscle of leading by building our capacity as listeners to our first stories from the Bible.

One of my mentors, the late Dallas Willard, repeatedly stated that the two most important questions we can ask of Christians today are, "What's your plan for discipleship?" and "How's that plan working?" If leaders are disciples, and leaders are planners, then this book is an attempt to help you map out strategically a plan for listening that is at the heart of great leadership. In Willard's teaching, you will have to "abstain" from some things in order to detach from their claims on your ear, mind, eye, and heart. Such *abstinence* then leads to time and space for disciplines of *engagement*, where we are free to truly hear and prepared to respond to God. God has a word worth hearing, and if you will learn to listen daily, it will help you with self-leadership and with leading others. This is how to optimize our opportunities and indeed our lives!

Methods

There are several ways to picture how we want to build this muscle for listening to God, leading others, and optimizing our lives. Here's one:

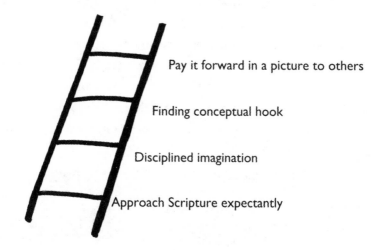

Pay it forward in a picture to others

Finding conceptual hook

Disciplined imagination

Approach Scripture expectantly

Here, we <u>plan</u> to come to the Bible every day out of confidence that it will be the most useful thing we can do as we prepare to lead. We come as part of the very rhythm of our life, like breakfast for our soul. Then, as we read with an eye for what God might say about leadership, we listen for a <u>hook,</u> a simple and straightforward word from God that emanates out of the characters, storyline, or direct teaching of the Scripture. Finally, as my friends in recovery say, "you can't keep it until you give it away." In other words, the leadership insights that come from the hook must be paid forward and passed along to someone else before they are fully activated in our own lives. Sharing what you have heard with someone else is the "activation code" or catalyst that brings the insight to life in leadership. Mastery comes through gifting to others.

I believe that the best way to do this is through a simple picture. Edward Tufte and Dan Roam have taught us that perhaps the best way to bring conceptual information to life and application is through simple, visual means. If you can't write it on the "back of a napkin," you haven't really absorbed the insight to the point where it is useful to you and others. Mike Breen, in using "LifeShapes," has understood this, and I have seen firsthand many times the power of a simple visual diagram to communicate vast leadership insights. Simple, visual information has the ability to be cross-cultural and multi-generational. It has the wherewithal to cut through the muck of words and get to the heart of action-oriented, mind-changing, behavior-modifying leadership.

Breen's triangle illustrates this:

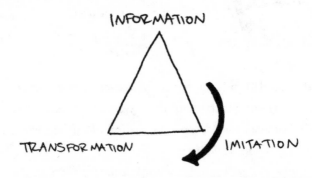

The great fallacy of how we grow is that we move straight from *Information* to *Transformation*. But "more informed" clearly does not automatically equate to "fully transformed." To get to *transformation*, one must first go through a process of *imitation*. We need models, mentors, demonstrations, living examples. We need people who can, step-by-step, show us how a word from God became part of our life, and how it can become a part of your life. This is why Paul repeatedly said to his young churches, *"Imitate me, just as I also imitate Christ"* (1 Corinthians 11:1). The Incarnation demonstrates that we need knowledge embodied, modeled, and lived out before it can become part of our way of being and doing. Only then does knowledge become wisdom and revelation:

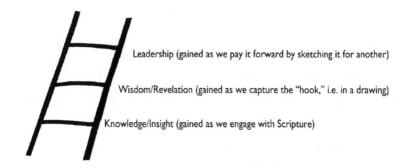

Leadership (gained as we pay it forward by sketching it for another)

Wisdom/Revelation (gained as we capture the "hook," i.e. in a drawing)

Knowledge/Insight (gained as we engage with Scripture)

So, while God will impress upon us great insights while we engage with Scripture, those insights do not become a part of our transformation until we capture and then pass them along. And we can pass them along by sketching them out for another person to receive in such a way that they, too, can pay it forward.

Again, I don't pretend to have come close to exhausting the insights available in these selected chapters. My aim is for this to be a how-to manual, not a coffee table book. Watch what I do here, and then imitate this habit in your own way. My hope is that you will learn to engage with Old Testament leaders in a way that informs the decisions you have to make every day as you lead people. My prayer is that, after practicing your way through this book, you will have built the muscles to do the work of mining on your own as you continue to excavate the Bible. I can promise that it will change you as a disciple and as a leader.

Operating Instructions: *How to use*

Before opening the Bible ...

Just do it. Begin the discipline of studying a chapter of the Bible a day on the very day you get this book. Don't procrastinate and don't try to wait until the beginning of a new book of the Bible or first day of the month or year.

Kneel. I suggest a beginning with a brief physical gesture, or ritual that will help you to put yourself in a posture of receiving. I use a kneeler bench outside of my bedroom door, so that before I walk out for the day, I have submitted to God for guidance. However you choose, ask God to open your heart to hearing as you submit yourself to the discipline of listening to the Bible.

Prepare your workspace. I find it very useful to have a certain desk where I do this work every day; it is part of a routine which helps form habit. It is a signal to my body and mind of what I am about to undertake. Bring with you a Bible you can write in, a pen, and a ruler. A notepad is useful for putting persistent distractions in a parking lot until later.

Plan. For me, writing key notes in a single Bible is useful. Working on a single chapter per day (or sometimes a slightly longer thought-unit) sets a consistent scope. Block off your daily calendar and notify those who need to know that you are unavailable during this time.

Win the first battle of the day. "Time" and "Space" are the media of creation in Genesis 1 and continue to be today. There will be a battle for your heart and for your attention. For me, I had to postpone reading two daily newspapers and discard *SportsCenter*. It will be vital to read the Bible before texts, email, Facebook, Twitter, etc. Turn the sound notifications off on all devices and resolve to open yourself to Scripture before engaging electronically.

While the Bible is open before you ...

Start with the Bible alone. Before looking at commentaries, annotations, or anything anyone else has said about the Scripture before you, give your chapter a chance to speak to you on its own terms. Read, re-read, and perhaps read aloud until you digest the chapter. I also practice by reading it in Spanish; if you know another language, use it to slow you down and think more richly about nuances.

Underline intuitively. When (re)reading the chapter of the day, highlight and underline intuitively. Where do words, phrases, sentences, verses, or even whole sections of Scripture jump off of the page at you? Don't over-think, but make notes of strong impressions.

Study alongside of church history. You can't know what the Bible means to me until you know what it meant to the people to whom it was written, and you can't know what the Bible meant until you actually listen to what it says. Beyond "impressionism" lays the rigorous examination of three thousand years of reflection by others who have engaged with the Bible. Pick a few trusted commentaries – and if you know don't whom to trust, ask someone who does – and let them serve as guides to help you listen to the Scripture. You don't want to do this *before* listening on your own to Scripture ... but you don't want to be the only one listening to the Scripture. For me, heroes like Walter Brueggemann are trustworthy guides to hearing the Bible on its own terms. Read what one or two commentaries say about your chapter. Take notes where the insights of others illumine your reading so that if you were to go back later to a page of Scripture, ideas for the interpretation of that passage would be on the page and ready to share.

Hone in. Now, after having used the wide-angle lens, narrow it back down. From your own impressions and from the insights gained by wider study, hone in on one focal verse. (At times, it may be a single word, the action of a character, or a short passage. Don't get too legalistic about it.) By this point, your underlining and notes will be great clues.

Receive again. As you hone in on your verse, ask God to reveal what he is trying to say about how you lead and how you might help others lead. This is what I mean by reading the Bible through the lens of leadership, and leadership through the lens of discipleship. Ask for a "word" from God. Using the key verse, ask the Lord to fix in your mind and heart for the day some divine direction or guidance. It may be as simple as a single word that you want to repeat throughout the day. Or, it could be a phrase, the verse itself, or illustration of a key story of the biblical text. Ask God for grace to remember and return to that word throughout that day. This is not hocus-pocus but more akin to Paul Ricoeur's "second naiveté."

After you have closed the Bible ...

Use "fresh bread." Before leaving the time and space of the "first battle of the day," commit to sharing in some venue (verbal or written) your received "word" from God (a verse/principle/story)

Praying New Beginnings

during same day that you received it. Resolve to share what you have heard and learned with someone in a situation that will become apparent to you only once you are in it. Don't cram or force it, but go into the day open to sharing what you yourself have heard from Scripture and how it is affecting you. As often as not, you will be giving testimony as to how God is changing you as a leader as you will be offering input to someone else about how they lead.

Draw it on the back of a napkin. We close the loop when we pay forward to someone else what God has offered to us. Do so by sharing the word you have received with a very simple illustration or diagram. Such a picture gives you ways to "operationalize" insights into active leadership practice and make it useful in daily life. It will not only potentially help a person you are trying to lead; it will also finish the circuit for your own absorption of the word from God in your life.

Genesis 1

"God saw everything that he had made, and indeed, it was very good." – Genesis 1:31

This may be the most important verse in the Bible.

Creation is the moment God ceased to be everything so that we could become something. Written during a time of Babylonian chaos to people who thought that life had no order, Genesis 1 promises that the world is in fact a symphony composed by the master conductor. It has theme and counterpoint, key and signature. Most of all, as it says again and again, creation has rhythm:

- *"And God said ..."*

- *And it was so ...*

- *And there was evening and morning, the (first through seventh) day."* (Repeat!)

Against the chaos of the times, the overture of the Bible is that life is not, in fact, chaotic. At the heart of things is purpose and rhythm. This is not a chronicle of archaeology; it is a poem about the way life in the world is and is meant to be: beautiful, unfolding, orderly, (but with delightful surprises), conducted.

Yes, creation (including humanity) will fall only two chapters later, disrupting the divine song. But leaders never forget that Genesis 1 comes before Genesis 3. We never forget that the creation is *"indeed very good"* and that the people we lead are made in the image of God. Before people are redeemed they must first be affirmed.

Jesus tells his disciple to *"Strive first for the kingdom of God and his righteousness, and all these things will be given to you as well"* (Matthew 6:33). The way Genesis 1 would affirm this is to say that the first order of a leader/disciple is to get in step with the rhythm of God. Life is music, the world is a poem, the people we lead are originally *very good*, and this dance is going somewhere. Lead with rhythm and in step with where God is going, and you will shape time, space, and history!

Exercise: *What or whom do you need to affirm as "indeed very good" today as you think about making decisions?*

Genesis 2

TILLING AND KEEPING THE GARDEN

"The Lord God took the man and put him in the garden of Eden to till it and keep it."
– Genesis 2:15

The second Genesis creation account is a commentary on the proper response to the divine symphony of creation. At the start of chapter 2, God's response to finishing creation is to *"bless"* it and to *"rest"* (vv. 2f). The Sabbath is an eternal gift and a reminder that creation and work are not ends in themselves, but are means to relationship, joy, gift, and blessing.

Praying New Beginnings

At the end of the chapter, the first man and woman are given in a *"one flesh"* relationship. Their first words in v. 23 are actually a song, a poem: *"This at lost is bone of my bones and flesh of my flesh ...!"* It is a picture of the interpersonal beauty toward which all creation aims. God created us for intimate relationship that is *"naked and not ashamed"* (v. 25).

So response to creation begins in the <u>rest</u> of Sabbath and culminates in the <u>relationship</u> of intimacy. In between is our assignment: to *"till and keep"* the Garden of Eden.

We have work to do – the work of tending the *"garden"* of God's creation. This work involves <u>tilling</u> (uprooting and disrupting) and <u>keeping</u> (conserving and nurturing). And the work of gardening is framed within the frame of rest and relationship, between the initiative of God and intimacy of human companionship. It is a work not of creation (God has already done that!) but cultivation.

A leader will do well to remember the foundation of rest, the landing place of intimacy, and the work of gardening as the core task of those s/he leads. When we *"till and keep"* people and teach them to do this same work of cultivating, we mimic the rhythm of creation and we work in the world's garden in the way it was meant to be.

Exercise: *Is your assignment today more about "tilling" or "keeping" the relationships around you?*

Genesis 3

"But the Lord God called to the man, and said to him,
"Where are you?" – Genesis 3:9

The story of our fall from the grace of gardening is the story
of our rejection of God's invitation, hospitality, and vocation. We
accept the analysis of a stranger ("*the serpent*") over the voice
of a friend. We reduce the vocation to "*till and keep the garden*"
(2:15) to the much-smaller world of whether to eat and what we

should consume (*"the fruit"*). We interpret God's prohibitions and boundaries (what not to eat) as his holding back from us, rather than as his gracious protection. What results from all of this is the distortion of *"desire"* (v. 16), the reduction of work into *"toil"* (v. 17), and the introduction of shame into the relational fabric of the world.

God steps in as a leader into this broken situation. Famously, God makes *"garments"* for Adam and Eve (v. 21), dealing with their shame when they are unable to do so. But before that, God forecasts how leadership always involves <u>intervention</u>. Though the man and woman are hiding in the garden (v. 8), God seeks out and addresses them: *"Where are you?"* God knows where they are, and knows that the situation is not pretty. Yet the work of a leader always involves asking that hard question of *"Where are you?"* to followers. It is a question that addresses difficult reality, confronts ugly situations, and begins the work of sorting out the mess.

It would be easier simply to avoid and evade the train-wrecks of those we lead (not to mention our own). But leadership means redemption through beginning with the question, *"Where are you?"* Leading begins with confronting brokenness head-on. Though it is often a painful question, it ignites the core conversation, and a leader can never be "above" conversation. For such conversation is the only path through which redemption travels.

Exercise. *Where are <u>you</u>? Is there someone today with whom you need to have a difficult or demanding conversation? Take a moment to reflect on who that might be. Rehearse a scenario of how you will approach them. And then pray for God to give you the grace and resolve to enter into the fray as a step toward restoration.*

Genesis 4

MASTERING THE LURKING BEAST

"If you do well, will you not be accepted? And if you do not do well, sin is lurking at the door; its desire is for you, but you must master it." – Genesis 4:7

If the great question of the Fall story of Genesis 3 is, *"Where are you?"* then the great question of the Genesis 4 Fall story is, *"Where is your brother?"* (v. 8). Of course, by the time Cain asks this question of God about his brother Abel, it is merely rhetorical. Already having devolved from hot-headed second-degree murder to cold-hearted first-degree murder, Cain *"rose up against his brother Abel, and killed him"* (v. 8). By the time Cain retorts to God, *"Am I my brother's keeper?"* (v. 9), it is not a serious question. His brother is already dead. It's a bit late for that question.

It is too late because Cain failed to address something more foundational. Furious at the inequity of life (and God), Cain's anger had welled up within him like a lion. The Lord, graciously, warned Cain. *"Sin,"* says God, is like a beast *"lurking at the door."* Animal-like, his anger crouched, looking for an opening to pounce inside. At that point, it could have been held at bay. Once it had a foot in the door, though, it was uncontrollable. The rest is bloody history.

The question, *"Am I my brother's keeper?"* is moot if you haven't first mastered the prior issue of the lurking beast at the gate. It is a visual of one of the grand themes of the Bible: unless we first address human sin, our hopes of do-gooding are tragically impossible. The hope of tranquil human harmony is merely wishful thinking if there's a roaring lion running around in our midst.

Before a leader's grand ambitions must come mastery on a very personal level. We have to deal with the sin *"lurking at our door."* It is possible to for us *"do well."* But it is not possible unless we first master the lurking beast.

Exercise: *What sin is lurking at your door today? Envision doing well to keep it at bay, mastering it and not allowing it a foot-hood in your life. Remember that temptation is not the same as sinning! Ask God for the vigilance to keep the danger away from your heart.*

WALKING WITH GOD
PART I

"Enoch walked with God; then he was no more, because God took him." – Genesis 5:24

After two stories of the Fall – the serpent in the Garden, and Cain murdering Abel – the next story of the Genesis of why things are the way they are lists ten men/generations between Adam and Noah. The only remarkable thing about each man is his fantastically high age of death – from ages 777 (Lamech) to 969 (Methuselah) years old. And within those ten is one even more remarkable, namely Enoch. His age at death is not listed because he is not recorded as having died at all. Instead, *"he was no more, because God took him."*

This has fueled centuries of speculation about what became of Enoch. The lens through which Christians interpret this is Hebrews 11:5, which says that Enoch *"did not experience death,"* having been taken away because *"he had pleased God."* Thus what is suggested in Genesis and clarified in Hebrews is that this human being, even after the Fall, experienced eternal life with God. And, his eternal life with God was connected with an earthly life of pleasing God by faith.

Paraphrasing Kierkegaard, people are not problems to be solved but mysteries to be explored. The great mystery of humanity and the greater gift of God is that ordinary, fallen mortals were created for eternity. We were made with the hope that, by faith, we might walk with God.

When leaders can look at others in this way, irritating and flawed as they might be, we can lead from an eternal perspective, and accomplish things of eternal worth.

Exercise: *Is there a difficult person with whom you are dealing right now that you can envision as "made for eternity?" Ask God to help you see them this way today.*

Genesis 6

WALKING WITH GOD
PART 2

Noah was a righteous man, blameless in his generation; Noah walked with God." – Genesis 6:9

Lest one think the chapter 5 story of Enoch was a one-off about heaven alone, the Bible follows up his account of *"walking with God"* with the story of Noah. *"Alone righteous before (God) in this generation"* (7:1), Noah embodies the first remnant of faithfulness in a more-wicked earth. With Noah, God makes the first relational *"covenant"* (v. 18) in the Bible.

In a *"corrupt"* (vv. 11-13) and violent earth, God asks Noah to build an embedded space and a contrast community. He is to build an ark as counter-testimony to the way things are, demonstrating instead the way things should be. The ark looks both like a coffin (John Calvin) and a cathedral (per Gothic architects). It represents life in the midst of death, righteousness in the middle of wickedness, covenant faithfulness floating over relational violence.

In building this ark, this counter-community, Noah *"walks with God."* Walking with God is not just something that you do after your earthly life (as with Enoch). It is in trajectory with how you live in this life (as with Noah). If you want to walk with God in heaven, better to begin practicing that walking here on earth.

Noah leads by beginning - right now! - to walk into the higher reality which will come one day. No leader should simply pine for the way things should be even as life falls far short of that right now. Instead, s/he begins to participate in the reality to which s/he points. We walk with God today as the dress rehearsal for the wedding of eternity itself!

Exercise: *What "heavenly" habit do you need to begin practicing immediately, beginning right now? Pray for the imagination and attentiveness to do that today.*

LEADING FROM THE MINORITY

"Then the Lord said to Noah, "Go into the ark, you and all your household, for I have seen that you alone are righteous before me in this generation." – Genesis 7:1

Eden is lost, Cain has murdered his brother, and "*the wickedness of humankind was great in the earth*" (6:5). All of this makes the Lord "*sorry that he had made humankind on the earth, and it grieved him to his heart*" (6.6). It also caused him to hit the re-set button and wash the earth clean in a flood – except for Noah and his tribe.

Noah is by no means perfect. He drank too much (9:20ff). But at this time, he is all that God has. Noah models human responsiveness and faithfulness in a minority setting. It's easy to lead when you're in Eden. But we're not in Eden anymore. And Noah is worthy of imitating because he figures out how to respond to God when no one else around him seems interested in doing that. In this way, he is the first in long line of faithful "remnant" leaders who do "*all that the Lord had commanded*" (v. 5) when it is decidedly unpopular to do so.

We are long past the day in the United States when the church is at the head of the table in a community conversation. Increasingly, the church is no longer even invited to the table; and at times, there are pickets outside protesting the presence of Christian leaders. Get over it. As Rick Warren says, "majority rules" are among the words never found in the Bible. Noah demonstrates that living righteously and leading in faith occur most pointedly when doing such is in sharp contrast to everyone and everything around you.

Prayer: *"God of heaven and earth, help me live and lead today for an audience of One. Help me to be responsive to you no matter the prevailing winds of opinion around me. Help me to take my cues from what you tell me and not from what I see in the majority. Grant me faithfulness, resolve, steadfastness, and a humble and obedient heart. In the name of Jesus, Amen."*

Genesis 8

RAVEN, DOVE, OLIVE LEAF, GONE

"At the end of forty days Noah opened the window of the
ark that he had made and sent out the raven ...."
– Genesis 8:6-7

The first half of the story of Noah demonstrates his leadership through obedience to God, even when in radically minority context. God gives him an incredible task – build a giant ark and gather pairs of every animal – and Noah listens to God so diligently that he and his family alone escape the flood.

The second half of the story, however, show Noah as a leader not simply in responsive obedience, but because he takes initiative

Praying New Beginnings

and is persistent and innovative. After the flood, Noah is not simply an order-taker. On his own, he sends out four progressive envoys to see if the time in the ark is ending:

Dove (doesn't return)

Dove (returns with olive leaf) →

Dove (returns empty) →

Raven →

Each attempt builds on the previous attempt. Like an observation-based scientist, Noah tries something, tweaks it, and repeats, until he gets the answer he is looking for. Once, he changes bird type. Another time, he goes with the already-experienced dove. As Jim Collins might later describe it in *Great By Choice*, Noah engages in "empirical creativity." He "first fires bullets, then cannonballs."

Sometimes, it is the task of the leader to wait patiently for God to give direct guidance, and to respond immediately and obediently when God does. At other times, though, the leader is to take initiative, experiment, observe, persist, innovate, and improve. We send out the raven, then the dove (repeatedly) until we get our answer. And in this way, we partner with God as leaders working in a re-set creation.

Exercise: *How can you "experiment" with a small change today in your decision-making? If the experiment doesn't work, do not lose heart. Persist in exploring possible paths for God's will. Be open and curious about it. When you find a way that bears fruit, then and only then follow it.*

Genesis 9

BE FRUITFUL,   MULTIPLY,   FILL THE EARTH

"God blessed Noah and his son, and said to them, "Be fruitful and multiply, and fill the earth." – Genesis 9:1

Putting his weapon down, God has undrawn his warrior's bow and transformed it into a rainbow of promise: *"I have set my bow in the clouds, and it shall be a sign of the covenant between me and the earth"* (v. 15). The flood has washed the earth of its pervasive evil, and now Noah and his clan are leaving the ark and preparing to live in a new day.

Praying New Beginnings

What are they to do? The order in verses 1 and 7 is the same order given to Adam and Eve in 1:28: *"Be fruitful and multiply, and fill the earth."* This is the archetypal command for those who would act as God's regents on the earth. Paul would later expound on the *"fruit of the Spirit" ("love, joy, peace,"* etc.) in Galatians 5:22. He would also spend his life multiplying churches, and fulfill the Acts 1:8 command to spread the love of God *"to the ends of the earth."* Jesus would instruct his followers to harvest the fruit of *"(making) disciples"* of *"all nations"* while filling the earth with the good news that *"remember, I am with you always"* (Matthew 28:19-20).

In each instance, we are to:

- **Be fruitful** – live internally in such a way that is outwardly obvious and life-giving;

- **Multiply** – not simply be self-contained but bring ourselves to bear on replicating that which is life-giving; and

- **Fill the earth** – not only be full of God's presence internally, but to live it out in such a way that the world around us becomes full of God's ruling presence.

Am I leading in such a way that the fruit of my life nourishes not only those around me but contributes toward none ever being hungry again? This is God's aim for leaders, for all those who will rule in a re-set earth.

Exercise: *Which of these three commands is most pertinent to me today? Am I to focus on upward "fruit" with God, inward "multiplying" of relational goodness, or outward "filling the earth" with justice and righteousness?*

Genesis 10

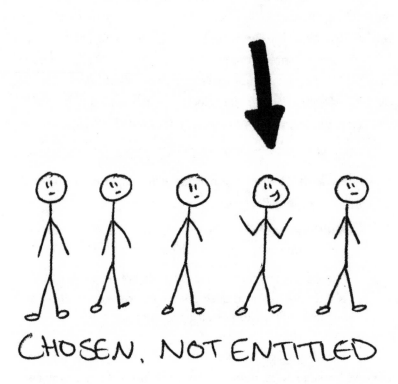

CHOSEN, NOT ENTITLED

"To Shem also, the father of all the children of Eber, the elder brother of Japheth, children were born."
– Genesis 10:21

Praying New Beginnings

Genesis 10 is "the table of the nations," intended to describe a reset population between Noah and Babel. For the most part, it is of interest only to scholars. Tucked away in the list, though, is the etymology of Israel – "*Shem*" (the Semites), *the father of all the children of Eber"* (the Hebrews).

It is a noteworthy detail that the people whom God chose to be his instruments in the world have unremarkable origins. They are not first (primary), middle (central), or last (ultimate) nation in the list. A point is being driven home: God's "chosen people" are not ontologically, intrinsically, or etymologically special. "*Shem*" and "*Eber*" are simply part of the larger human family, and not a particularly remarkable part at that. The Hebrew people become the protagonists of the Old Testament because God selected or chose them, not because of any inherently distinguishing characteristic.

What is true of the Hebrews is true of all of us: we are what we are because of the grace of God. To any whose heads might swell with an overly high self-assessment of our irreplaceability, this is a reminder that we are chosen, not entitled. We are "special" only inasmuch as God has deemed us to be chosen instruments in the grand story of history. There is no room for us to swell with undue pride, only responsive gratitude. *"Amazing grace, how sweet the sound, that saved a wretch like me!"*

Exercise: *Reflect on this amazing grace: that long before you chose God, God chose you. Pause to give thanks for the reality that God loves you intrinsically, apart from your performance or ability. Dwell in that grace until it overflows on your interactions with others today.*

"And the Lord said, "Look, they are one people, and they have all one language; and this is only the beginning of what they will do; nothing that they propose to do now will be impossible for them." – Genesis 11:6

The Mesopotamians and Incas had their ziggurats, stairways to heaven. The Greeks followed the myth of Prometheus, driven by hopes for the security, unity, and fame of humanity. And the Bible has the story of "*Babel*," the "Gate of God" – the story of how God frustrated yet another human attempt to overreach our mortality and finitude.

Genesis 1-11 has described the alienation of husband and wife (Adam and Eve), brothers (Cain and Abel), and children and parents (Noah and his sons). Now it describes why the peoples don't get along and don't "*have all one language.*" We are "confused" ("*Babel*" is a pun on the Hebrew word, "*balal,*" meaning "confuse") because if we all spoke the same language, we would be far more efficient in destroying the world we intended to save. God's move to "*confuse the language of all the earth*" and "*scatter them abroad*" (v. 9) is an act of divine intervention to frustrate our overly-optimistic aspirations of city-building and tower-making. God the Father takes the lighter away from the toddler.

Leaders must remember that our own unchecked power is not a good thing. We can be very earnest and very wrong. What we sometimes experience as frustration and confusion in reaching our aspirations can instead be the loving grace of God reaching down to stop us from accomplishing the things we intend because they will do great harm.

The way of human ambition is finally shown to be "*barren*" (v. 30). The way of divine grace will be seen through God calling us to bless the earth, not build a tower. And our responsiveness to that holy calling, not our aspirations to "*build ourselves a city, and a tower with its top in the heavens*" (v. 4), will be the path to blessing the creation.

Exercise: *In what ways am I ambitious? Am I aspiring to build a "city" or "tower?" Are there costs associated with this? Reflect on what is frustrating your ambitions to see if there might be grace involved.*

Genesis 12

BLESSED TO BLESS

"Now the Lord said to Abram, "Go from your country and your kindred and your father's house to the land that I will show you. I will make you a great nation ... and in you all the families of the earth shall be blessed." – Genesis 12:1-3

Praying New Beginnings

Creation has hit rock bottom, tumbling from the serpent, to Cain, the Flood, and finally Babel. The human project to build and inhabit the earth is finally *"barren"* (11:30). There is no future.

But just as God once created something out of *"formless void and darkness"* (1:2) and brought order into chaos when he said, *"Let there be light"* (1:3), so now again God makes something out of nothing. God calls Abram. The Lord chooses a people to represent his unique way as a minority witness in the world. God gives an assignment, a journey, a path which departs from the security and comfort of *"country, kindred, and father's house."* It is fraught with uncertainty.

But it is the path to blessing. And not simply the blessing of Abram, though that is involved. And not just the blessing of his *"nation,"* though that too happens. The key to God's new creation through calling servants to journey is that through Abram and his descendants, *"all the families of the earth shall be blessed."* Abram is blessed to be a blessing to others.

He often forgets this – like eight verses later, when he is willing to throw his wife Sarai under the bus and lie to the Egyptians in order to preserve his own hide. The desire for security is powerful and a serious deterrent to trust and journey. But at his best, Abram goes with God, represents God as his agent, is blessed, and becomes the agent of blessing in the world.

We who are called by God to lead will face the same temptations toward security, self-preservation, and the old impulse of city-building. But when we respond to the diving call and learn to be agents who intend to bless *"all the families of the earth,"* we become part of the healing and repair of God's new creation.

John P. Chandler 43

FAILURE TO DEFER

"So Lot chose for himself all the plain of the Jordan, and Lot journeyed eastward; thus they separated from each other."
– Genesis 13:11

Abram was a God-called leader who sought guidance continually: *"Abram called on the name of the Lord"* (v. 4). When Lot's father died, Abram took him under his wing. Lot had many servants and animals because his Godgiven leader was so good to him.

Prosperity led to a need for their tribes to spread out and separate. Legally and by custom, Abram was the leader. He had the right to choose the best land for himself. Lot should have asked Abram what he wanted. But Lot did not feel he owed anything to the one who had led him through difficult famine years and times of wandering.

Unlike Abram, Lot doesn't *"call on the name of the Lord"* about the decision. Failing to defer, he just grabs what he wants and leaves the one who loved him in the dust. Lot refuses to listen to Abram about how dangerous Sodom was. It looked good to his inexperienced eye. He didn't need some so-called "man of God" to tell him what to do. The outcome is historic strife between the descendants of Abram and descendants of Lot.

Refusing to work with God-given leaders bears deep consequences. Many a great journey and partnership has sadly unraveled because of failure to defer to a proper leader. When our ego gets in the way of proper deference, impulsive, egocentric decision-making is sure to follow. And so is relational strife, opportunity lost, and unnecessary destruction.

Exercise: *To whom should I show proper deference? What leaders deserve my respect, and how do I acknowledge and honor their place? Identify one such leader whom you will encounter today, and one long-term leader, and ask God to show you how to honor their leadership.*

Genesis 14

GIVING
ONE-TENTH

"He blessed him and said,"Blessed be Abram by God Most
High, maker of heaven and earth; and blessed be God Most
High, who has delivered your enemies into your hand! And
Abram gave him one-tenth of everything."
– Genesis 14:19-20

Abram is a peaceful and prosperous man, but there is a time
when even the peaceful and prosperous have to fight. Abram has
taken up arms to rescue his (selfish and ungrateful) nephew Lot.
The mission was successful. And now, *"King Melchizedek of Salem*

("Shalom") ... *priest of the Most High"* (v. 18) pronounces a blessing on Abram, and blesses God, the source of Abram's deliverance.

Abram's response is to give to the priest of "*one-tenth of everything,"* or the "tithe." He is then extremely generous in his interactions with the king of Sodom (vv. 22-24). These acts of generosity are ways that a powerful and victorious man acknowledges his dependence on others. The gifts are concrete expressions of humility. They re-set perspective decisively. The tithe and the gifts that follow reframe a blessed person from thinking he deserves and has earned what he has into a person who acknowledges God as the source of blessing. It causes him to treat others open-handedly. Abram doesn't gloat; he gives.

Giving "*one-tenth*" of what you have on a regular basis will do this. A leader can only call on others to give what s/he has first been willing to give. The amount doesn't matter, but the proportion does. The genius of the tithe is that it models not equal giving but equal sacrifice. Once you tithe, you will almost inevitably go beyond "*one-tenth*" to even greater generosity in your interactions.

If you lead, the precedent of Abram (later affirmed by Jesus in Matthew 23:23) is to tithe. It is better than money in the bank: if tithing becomes a habit, it will be more than a source of blessing to others. It will transform you into a humble, grateful, open-handed, generous leader.

Exercise: *Am I on a path toward becoming a more generous person? Where do I fit on the "tithing" spectrum: ignoring it, working toward it, practicing it, moving beyond it? Ask God to work in your heart toward more intentional and responsive generosity.*

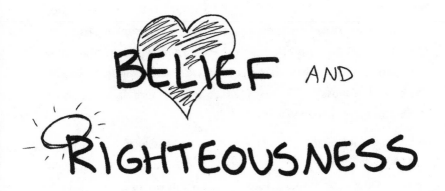

"And he believed the Lord; and the Lord reckoned it to him as righteousness." **– Genesis 15:6**

Abram is fearful and can't see the future path: *"the word of the Lord came to Abram in a vision, "Do not be afraid"* (v. 1).

He has serious questions, given the evidence, about how the future is going to work out: *"But Abram said, "O Lord God, what will you give me, for I continue childless …?"* (v. 2)

He is vulnerable, on a journey in foreign territory, getting no younger, and needs reassurance of protection and promise. And so the Lord says, *"Do not be afraid, Abram, I am your shield; your reward shall be very great"* (v. 1b).

All he has, really, is a willingness to believe God in the face of countering evidence – ongoing childlessness, vulnerability as a sojourner, the clock ticking. This willingness to believe God, though, is apparently enough. When Abram *"believed the Lord,"* then *"the Lord reckoned it to him as righteousness."* *"Believed"* connotes images of nourishment (as in a nursing mother) and support (as in the pillar of a building). Abram looks to God as his source of nourishment and support, and in response, God cut a covenant with Abram. With blood and fire, God visibly ratifies all that he has verbally promised. Things are now set right between God and Abram – *"the Lord reckoned it to him as righteousness."* And it is enough for Abram to go on.

Belief is a powerful thing. It can overcome fear, defy the odds, and secure perseverance. But more than belief itself, belief in the right God – the God of the Bible – can set things right. Such belief is more than subjective reassurance. It is beyond talking yourself into something you don't really think is going to happen. Belief in the God of the Bible is the way to set things right in your relationship with the objective God of the universe who is in charge of the way things are going to go in the future. When you are in right relationship with *that* God, you are going to be okay!

Exercise: *As a way of working out your muscles of "belief" today, reflect on the ways in which God has <u>nourished</u> you, and the ways God has <u>supported</u> you. Is God, even now, being tender with you as a nurse, and as strong for you as a pillar? Meditate on God's goodness to you.*

Genesis 16

THE COSTS
OF IMPATIENCE

"He shall be a wild ass of a man, with his hand against everyone, and everyone's hand against him; and he shall live at odds with his kin." – Genesis 16:12

Perhaps because "*a deep and terrifying darkness descended upon him*" (15:12 – Depression? Anxiety? The dark night of the soul?), Abram found the reassurances of God cutting a covenant to be not quite enough. He's eighty-six, childless, and has been waiting forever (it seems) for God to deliver on the promise of an heir. He feels he must secure his future; he cannot wait on God forever.

Praying New Beginnings

And so, just as Adam mutely followed Eve in the garden, so now Abram quietly gives in to the temptations offered by his wife, Sarai. She gives him Hagar *"as a wife"* (v. 3). She is her *"Egyptian slave girl"* (those three words in ancient Israel are strikes one, two, and three). No more does Abram *"call on the name of the Lord"* (13:2). Now he passively follows his angry and frustrated wife. Thinking he is taking matters into his own hands as a leader, he is really only following her.

Hagar subsequently gives birth to *"Ishmael"* and the conflict that ensues between Hagar, Sarai, and Abram is only a tiny foretaste of trouble to come. Ishmael *"shall live at odds with his kin,"* and not just for one generation. Tensions will be played out in the lives of Jacob and Esau, Israel and her Arab neighbors, and in the Middle East as recently as this morning.

Some leaders, thinking it demonstrates their initiative, vigor, and "take-charge" attitude, proudly declare their own impatience. But impatience is like a mutual fund with a back-end commission. It is a layaway purchase charging exorbitant interest rates. Its costs are borne far beyond the immediate circumstance. At its core, impatience demonstrates lack of faith, an unwillingness to wait on and fully trust in God.

Being impatient is nothing to brag about. When you create an Ismael because you can't wait on an Isaac, the costs can be exorbitant. Impatience will erode your faith in God, and destroy relational capital in your life and in generations to come.

Exercise: *Am I more likely tempted today simply to follow someone mutely and unreflectively, or to take matters into my own hands impatiently and preemptively?*

ALTERED

IDƎNTITY

"No longer shall your name be Abram, but your name shall be Abraham; for I have made you the ancestor of a multitude of nations. I make you exceedingly fruitful ... As for Sarai your wife, you shall not call her Sarai, but Sarah shall be her name. I will bless her ...." – **Genesis 17:5, 15-16**

A covenant is a relationship between a stronger and weaker party, ratified in blood (in chapter 15, by animal sacrifice, and in chapter 17, with circumcision). God graciously offers a covenant relationship to Abram and Sarai, signifying God's willingness to die in order to protect his human partners. (The rest of that story will only be told at the cross.)

Praying New Beginnings

In the covenant, "*God Almighty*" takes his name, which in Hebrew is written, "*YHWH*" (there are consonants only in Hebrew). Ancient rabbis who expounded this text point out that when the Hebrew says, "*I will make you the ancestor of many nations*" it is suggesting, "I will give you a letter from my name." So God gives Abram one "H" and Sarai gets the other "H" from the divine name. Their names are changed, an "H" is added, their identities become new, and their futures are blessed.

When the covenant is made, partners actually get a piece of God, component of his name. We are given the gift of being able to partake in the life of heaven, which alters our life irrevocably. This is why Paul would later tell new Christians, "*Set your minds on things that are above, not on things that are on earth, for you have died, and your life is hidden with Christ in God*" (Colossians 3:2-3). We are, in our baptismal covenant, able to claim a new identity as a gift of God through Christ.

God our leader has, in Christ, offered us a covenant of relationship which changes how we think of ourselves and how we are called by others. Whatever our previous identity, we now have a new identity! A new and fruitful future is open to us. And the story of our leadership is the ongoing story how we live and lead out of this new identity.

Exercise: *Reflect on the identity God has given you in your baptism, where God said to you, "You are my beloved, in whom I am well-pleased." Relish that gift of identity and the future that is open to you as you live and lead out of it!*

John P. Chandler

"(Abraham) looked up and saw three men standing near him. When he saw them, he ran from the tent entrance to meet them, and bowed down to the ground. He said, "My lord, if I find favor with you, do not pass by your servant. Let a little water be brought, and wash your feet, and rest yourselves under the tree. Let me bring a little bread, that you may refresh yourselves ...." – Genesis 18:2-5

In this famous instance of entertaining angels unaware, Abraham demonstrates classic Middle Eastern courtesy and hospitality. Like the father in Jesus' parable of the prodigal son (Luke 15), Abraham *"ran"* out, killed a fatted calf, and in almost embarrassing generosity extends his protection, company, and household resources for the benefit of strangers passing by. The *"little bread"* and *"little water"* are like sacraments of hospitality and feasting.

Good move! The strangers turn out to be bearers of unbelievable news. Because he has extended generous hospitality to the Lord himself, Abraham is then made privy to the future God is about to unfold. And, shockingly, he later gets to enter into a dialogue with God that actually shapes the course of the future, bargaining God down from fifty to ten on the matter of Sodom and Gomorrah (vv. 22-23). God honors Abraham as a conversation partner about shaping the future of nations.

Showing hospitality to others is a path to receiving hospitality from God. Jesus said that when we show hospitality to the *"least of these"* we actually draw nearer to him (Matthew 25:31-46). Xenophobia is not only a bad national policy; fear of the stranger is also a cramp for your soul.

Exercise: *In what ways can I practice hospitality today? How can I be more hospitable to strangers, particularly? What would growth in hospitality look like in my life?*

THE OPPOSITE OF
HOSPITALITY

"But before they lay down, the men of the city, the men of Sodom, both young and old, all the people to the last man, surrounded the house; and they called to Lot, "Where are the men who came to you tonight? Bring them out to us, so that we may know them." Lot went out of the door to the men, shut the door after him, and said, "I beg you, my brothers, do not act so wickedly." – Genesis 19:4-7

Abraham's nephew Lot echoes his uncle's hospitality to strangers and welcomes angels unaware. But he is complete outlier in the city. Without exception, every other man in Sodom wants to show the opposite of hospitality: they want to take advantage of the visiting strangers. Instead of lavishing generosity upon them, they press to ravish them sexually.

Rape is the sacrament of evil and the opposite of hospitality. It acts out domination over mutuality, robbery over sanctuary, attack over welcome and protection. Sodom and Gomorrah are finally destroyed not only because of their perversity, but because of the wanton preference for rape over hospitality.

Lot is spared while the city is destroyed by God, forecasting the final destruction of all such evil when God ultimately reconciles accounts. But neither do Lot and his family escape judgment, because they "*linger*" (v. 16) and "*looked back*" (v. 26) permissively on a city and culture of rape. It is just as impermissible to tolerate a culture of rape as it is to enact it. The opposite of hospitality is not an offense of etiquette but a crime against God and humanity, and cannot be tolerated by God or by us.

Prayer: *"Lord, let me never be willing to tolerate the intolerable. Forgive my quietude in the face of the violence and violation done to those around me who are overpowered sexually. Walk with those in our community who live daily in the aftermath of this hurt. And give me a voice to cry out against every culture of rape that I encounter, in the name of Jesus, Amen."*

UNWORTHY BUT
NECESSARY LEADERS

"Then Abraham prayed to God, and God healed Abimelech, and also healed his wife and female slaves so that they bore children." **– Genesis 20:17**

In spite of witnessing the fearsome judgment of God on the wicked cities Sodom and Gomorrah, Abraham's next actions display a kind of duplicity unfitting for a spiritual leader. As in chapter 12, he tries to pass off his wife Sarah as a sister in order to avoid conflict with king Abimilech. When the king is told by God in a dream of the real situation, he is mortified and asks Abraham incredulously how he could have done this. What follows from Abraham is a series of half-baked excuses and double-talk.

The situation is then resolved, mostly because of the king's kindness and relief at his moral *"exoneration"* (v. 16). At that point, the story takes a surprising turn: it is Abraham who prays to God for the healing and fruitfulness of the king, and not the other way around. And God answers that prayer.

Like the people of God ever since, Abraham is unworthy, but is the vessel of life for the nations (12:3). Thank goodness that the promise of God rests on God and not on his agents! It is the authority of the Promise-giver and not the Promise-bearer that finally carries weight.

This is incredible good news for leader. Our moral character really does matter; it can deeply hinder or aid the work we are called to do. But the good news is that God is at work in the world to bless his people and uses us to do so. Augustine said, "The bird does not have to be as pretty as the song it sings." God writes straight with crooked lines! By grace, God uses unworthy but necessary leaders to be his ambassadors for blessing.

Prayer: *"God, accept my most profound and humble thanksgiving that you know me as I truly am, with all of my darkness, brokenness, and not-yet-ness – and yet you continue to love me, utilize me, and call me. Help me to trust your judgment of me over my own self-appraisal. And help me to be a blessing to pray for and serve others, in your name, Amen."*

Genesis 21

GOD AND EMOTIONS

"Now Sarah said, "God has brought laughter for me."
– Genesis 21:6

"The matter was very distressing for Abraham on account of his son." – Genesis 21:11

"As she sat down opposite of him, she lifted up her voice and wept." – Genesis 21:16

Genesis 21 is a collection of stories: the birth of Isaac, the dismissal of Hagar and Ishmael, and tension and covenant between Abraham and Abimilech. These are stories of high emotion: from the exuberant laughter of Sarah and feasting of Abraham (vv. 6-8), to the distress and weeping of Hagar as she is exiled to the desert to watch her son die (vv. 12, 16), to the tense negotiations between two alpha males (vv. 25ff). Reading the stories consecutively gives the effect of jerking one around emotionally, helping us to identify with the high sense of drama in the storyline.

How does God interact with the emotional extremes demonstrated by the characters in the story?

- God's actions elicit emotional response (v. 6), sometimes extreme;
- God proceeds with the story in spite of high emotions (v. 12);
- Yet God remains responsive and sensitive to the emotional responses of his people (v. 17).

In short, high emotions are noteworthy. They may affect the storyline, but they don't finally determine it.

A godly leader will respond to the emotional climate of those s/he leads in the same way. We are to pay attention when there is strong emotion around us. They affect us and we address them. They can sometimes be clues as to the shape of the story, and other times clues to the true inner landscape of our people. Yet at the end of the day, we have a mission to undertake, and nothing, including high emotion can ultimately be allowed to derail that. Change the pace, sometimes. But we ultimately have to lead through the turbulence of emotional range.

Exercise: *Journal your emotional highlights at the end of the day. As you audit these, take note of your own range, and the emotional range of those with whom you have interacted. Take stock of how you responded to the peaks and valleys, and ask God to give you intentionality as you encounter the emotional highs and lows in days to come.*

GOD WILL PROVIDE

"Abraham said, "God himself will provide the lamb for the burnt offering, my son." – Genesis 22:8

This fearsome story moves from God as "tester" to God as "provider." Like Adam in the garden of Eden and Jesus in the garden of Gethsemane, Abraham is placed under trial go see if he will remain obedient under duress. It illustrates that we often do not know what we are made of until we are placed in extreme situations.

In the course of his testing, Abraham offers one of the richest lines in all of Scripture: *"God himself will provide the lamb for a burnt offering, my son."* How could he have known that God would not only be faithful to give him a ram in the thicket for this offering, but that one day, God would provide *himself* for the offering, in the person of Jesus? Here, God provides for a son; later, God provides his only Son. Here, there is wood for the altar; there, on the cross, the wood becomes the altar.

One might go as far as to say that these two stories — the (near) sacrifice of Isaac and the completed sacrifice of Jesus — speak to the deepest mystery of the Bible. They show that, even and especially in the face of death, *"God himself will provide."*

Karl Barth said that *"provide"* is from *"pro-video"* — to see before, to anticipate, and to make arrangements ahead so that all will be cared for. God sees ahead to provide, even in the face of death.

A biblical leader never, ever, loses sight of this core truth. *God will provide.* We work alongside of God. We obey our call, even and especially in deeply distressing circumstances. We lead as if it is all up to us. But we never forget that it is God who will provide. God provided for Abraham and his descendants, and God provided for the world through Jesus Christ. And God will provide for you.

Exercise: *At the beginning and end of the day, give thanks to God for the concrete ways in which you have experienced his care and provision for you. Ask God in prayer for the ability to trust more deeply.*

ALIENS AND
PRINCES

"Abraham said ... I am a stranger and an alien residing among you ..." – **Genesis 23:3f**

"The Hittites answered Abraham, "Hear us my lord; you are a mighty prince among us." – **Genesis 23:5f**

The death of Sarah, Abraham's wife, provided one of those milepost moments in which a person assesses the core meaning of their life and identity. Abraham wants to purchase at full price a burial place that will be an abiding symbol of the Promised Land to come, even if that cave is in a foreign land. As he mourns and negotiates, he takes stock of who he is and who Sarah was, and how they want to be remembered.

He claims an identity as a *"stranger and alien residing"* in Canaan. He is with the Hittites but not one of them; among them but not like them; relationally connected to them but not holding to their nation as the core of his personhood. The burial cave will symbolize the meaning of Abraham and Sarah's lives – in but not of the world, missionaries connected relationally but distinct spiritually, bridges between where the people are and where, by grace, they might be. As Paul would later describe his ministry among the then-pagan Corinthians, *"Indeed, this is our boast, the testimony of our conscience: we have behaved in the world with frankness and godly sincerity, not by earthly wisdom but by the grace of God – and all the more toward you"* (2 Corinthians 1:12).

A leader must always dance to be enough like the people s/he leads to be highly regarded by them. But this connectedness must never corrupt their identity as leaders of a mission. In Genesis 23 language, leaders must be as well thought of as *"mighty princes"* but remember their identity as *"strangers and aliens residing among you"* – people with a mission to lead those among whom they dwell.

Exercise: *In what ways would it be best today if I functioned as a "stranger and alien," connected with but different from those around me?*

GOD- GIVEN RELATIONSHIPS

"As for me, the Lord has led me on the way to the house of my master's kin." – Genesis 24:27

With Sarah dead and Abraham's end approaching, the time to find a wife for their only son Isaac was job one. The selection of the right spouse was critical for the mission of preserving a people who were to be a unique blessing to the world. Abraham's servant is sent with elaborate instructions about what to say, where to go, to whom to listen, and how to respond in order to discern a successful match.

Just beneath the surface of the entire story is the conviction that God will provide the right relational connections. God will put the right people in the right places to have the right conversations leading to the right invitations and connections. The story plays out in meeting, courting, and winning Rebekah as a wife for Isaac. Again and again, the Lord is credited for making *"his journey successful"* (vv. 21, 56), showing *"steadfast love"* (v. 14), having *"led me on the way to the house"* (v. 27) and *"by the right way"* (v. 48). Everyone understands that the networking is providential. Even shifty uncle Laban has to admit, *"The thing comes from the Lord"* (v. 50).

Leaders are initiators who have to make things happen. We hustle to network, to put ourselves in position to meet the right people and have the right conversations. But one of the most proactive things we can do is to ask God to put us in place where these connections happen, and to give us minds to discern the answers to these prayers as they are happening. God works in mysterious ways, and some of those ways involve how we are providentially placed in the presence of game-changing relationships.

Exercise: *Pray today for God to put a key relationship in your path. Open your heart to the serendipity that comes when our initiative intersects with God's providence. At the end of the day, review the conversations of the day and give thanks for the gift of God's involvement in your networking.*

Genesis 25

"Esau said to Jacob, "Let me eat some of that red stuff, for I am famished ..." Jacob said, "First sell me your birthright." Esau said, "I am about to die; of what use is a birthright to me?" ... So he swore to him and sold his birthright to Jacob ....Thus Esau despised his birthright." – **Genesis 25:30-34**

After the death of Abraham, Genesis skips rapidly over the almost-mute son Isaac and straight into the story of grandson Jacob. (In terms of the leadership storyline, some leaders matter more than others.) Born as a twin grabbing his brother Esau, Jacob's life and leadership will be marked with trickery, conflict – and yet blessing.

But the first story is about Esau, Jacob's older brother and Isaac's rightful heir. A simple outdoorsman, Esau's defining moment is about how he gave away his right to lead. Starving after a hunt, smelling a pot of Jacob's *"lentil stew"* (v. 34), Esau impulsively traded away his right to lead to satisfy the cravings of an empty belly. He got what he wanted in the moment, and lost everything he was born to do. Even today, we should have rightly referred to "the God of Abraham, Isaac, and Esau." But Esau forfeited that right.

And, sadly, so have leaders ever since. All sorts of hungers (especially sexual hunger) have been the occasion of leaders handing over their authority to lead. Esau's decision should cause every one of us to pause and to count the long-term costs of giving in to temporary hungers.

The good news is that it is possible to resist the urges, instincts, and the pull of transient desires. Jesus, by overcoming the devil's temptation to *"turn stones into bread"* (Luke 4:3-4), paved the way for us to hold onto the long view and avoid disqualifying ourselves for our mission. To do so, we, like Jesus, must be disciplined, alert, and armed with a ready response to inevitable temptation. Arm yourselves, get that better script ready, and be prepared to answer the challenges that will surely come!

Exercise: *What is your "red stuff" or "lentil stew?" What are the things that tempt you and threaten to derail your mission? Is it a particular relationship? A particular habit or bodily need? What is available to you but should not be part of your life? Today, a). write down a word or name that captures this; b). tell a trusted friend that it is an area of temptation and ask for their support; in particular, ask them to ask you about it from time to time; and c). pray for God to make you alert when potential disrupters come, and give you strength to withstand them.*

Genesis 26

CONSERVATIVE LEADERSHIP

"Isaac dug again the wells of water that had been dug in the days of his father Abraham; for the Philistines had stopped them up after the death of Abraham; and he gave them the names that his father had given them." – Genesis 26:18

In the sweeping stories of the patriarchs and matriarchs, Isaac barely gets a speaking part. His basic charge comes in the first words God spoke to him: *"Do not go down to Egypt; settle in the land that I will show you*" (v. 2). In short, "Don't mess it up. Do as you are directed." Isaac was not to be a pioneering, innovative leader. His main charge was to bridge between his father Abraham and son Jacob.

In that vein, the main recorded story about Isaac's life describes his work of unstopping wells that enemies had spitefully filled up after the death of Abraham. Isaac re-dug and re-named those same wells, renewing sources of precious water in the desert.

In carrying out this task, Isaac demonstrates a classic form of the best conservative leadership. It is not his to create brilliant new ideas; he is to steward and renew the oldest dream of God's people that had been passed along by his father, Abraham. It was a dream that was in danger of drying up as the generation passed, and Isaac's work was to do the unglamorous work of opening up those old, life-giving waters for the people of his own day. Isaac was called to be a settler, not a pioneer. Some leaders clear new land, and others farm it. Isaac was to conserve what his father had known so that his own children could know it as well.

Perhaps pioneering leaders would do well to learn from Isaac's example. Sometimes the charge is not to pursue a wild new dream, but to restore an older dream for a newer generation.

Exercise: *Think specifically of an honorable legacy passed along to you from someone in the generation ahead of you. Meditate on what you must do to ensure that this same legacy will be handed down to someone specific in a generation that comes after you. As you picture specific representatives of these two generations, see yourself as a bridge between them. And ask God to reveal to you something that you need to do in order to see that legacy cross over that bridge.*

Genesis 27

"Isaac answered Esau, "I have already made him your lord, and I have given him all his brothers as servants, and with grain and wine I have sustained him. What then can I do for you, my son?" – Genesis 27:37

There are many powerful story lines in Jacob deceiving his father Isaac on his deathbed to steal Esau's blessing:

- Problems within families have long-term consequences.

- God sometimes chooses to bless in surprising ways.

- Emotional pleas can be "too little, too late."

One of the most powerful themes is the idea that a spoken blessing, like a gun fired, releases an un-retractable force. Once tricked, Isaac could not take back his blessing to Jacob and hand it over to Esau. There was no "re-do." The parent could not fix it. Esau pleads, *"Have you only one blessing, father? Bless me, me also, father!"* But Esau is not met with his father's blessing, only an *"answer"* (v. 39f). There is nothing left but regret, lament, and fury.

Among other things, it is a powerful reminder that certain words at critical times really, really matter. In "juncture" situations – in this case, at the hand-off of blessings and curses from one generation to the next – what you say can't be taken back. Once you say it, it stays said. It is part of the narrative from here on out.

Jesus said, *"On the day of judgment you will have to give an account for every careless word you utter; for by your words you will be justified, and by your words you will be condemned"* (Matthew 12:36f). A leader must remember that s/he has a stewardship of language. Our words represent not only our own fleeting feelings, but can be determinative and permanent, not only for ourselves but for many. That over which we speak blessing or cursing will be indelibly marked. Words already spoken cannot be undone.

Prayer: *"God, give me today a sense of the power of the words that I will speak. Grant me the wisdom to know what and whom to bless and to withhold blessing. Fill me with a sense of stewardship for my language, so that I may lead with honor, in the name of Jesus, Amen."*

Genesis 28

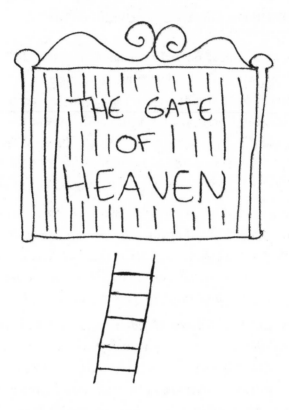

"Surely the Lord is in this place – and I did not know it! And he was afraid, and said, "How awesome is this place! This is none other than the house of God, and this is the gate of heaven." – **Genesis 28:16-17**

In a "thin place" between heaven and earth, unguarded and unsuspecting, God comes to Jacob in a dream. Sometimes these are the only times when we are quiet and still enough to hear from heaven.

Praying New Beginnings

Jacob dreams the opposite of Babel (Genesis 11). Instead of a human tower rising from earth, an angelic ladder descends from heaven. We don't climb to God; heaven comes down to us. No more fast running and fast talking for slick Jacob; God is the actor in this encounter, Jacob the receptor. And what God speaks to the rascal Jacob is blessing, promise, presence, protection, and covenant.

Jacob's response is to name the moment and place as holy (v. 16). He shows appropriate reverence at the fearsomeness of his encounter with the divine (v. 17). And he consecrates an altar or sanctuary, where he and many others after him will make important vows and gifts to this God (vv. 18-22).

Don't buy all of the pantheistic blather you hear about God being in every rock and insect. Some places are more important than others. Some moments are more holy than others. It is grace that God can and does break in to us in otherwise ordinary places and times. But it is also our work to build altars and sanctuaries where we ritualize, remember, and anticipate encounter with God and our responses.

You never know when and where God will show up. But you can build a *"pillar"* and pour *"oil on the top of it"* (v. 19) in disciplined anticipation of and response to the *"gate of heaven."* These spiritual markers define who we are and where we are going.

Exercise: *Pause now to remember several of the defining encounters with God in your life. Chart a simple timeline of them. Mark the moments. As you see the overview of these spiritual markers, humbly ask God for the grace to be open to his next step on the "ladder" from heaven to your life, whenever and wherever that might be.*

John P. Chandler

"This is not done in our country – giving the younger before the firstborn." – Genesis 29:26

Jacob runs for his life from the older brother Esau whom he has tricked. He lands in the fields of his uncle Laban and soon finds out what it means to be on the business end of being tricked. Falling in love with Laban's younger daughter on sight, Jacob is conscripted into seven years of service, only to be fooled on his wedding night with a substitute bride. The irony is in-your-face. And the whole setup is a recipe for all kinds of family drama for generations to come.

There is a noteworthy line uttered by Laban and a noteworthy act by Jacob that define the story. First, when Jacob protests that he should be free to marry the younger daughter Rachel instead of older Leah, Laban insists that such a thing *"is not done in our country."* First-born is first, oldest is strongest, eldest is best. It is only fair.

But while deceived here, Jacob is the person of power in the story. Though tricked into extra labor, he has the power to roll *"the stone from the well's mouth, and (water) the flock"* (v. 10) of the one who tricked him. It is a signal that there is power centered in this one who overcomes the rules of fairness. We get a glimpse of the great grace of God breaking through, a celebration of the awesome might of a way that is even greater than mere first-come-first-served fairness.

We instinctively prefer fairness to unfairness, and most of interpersonal life is built on that premise. But fairness itself is not our final hope. Ultimately, if we only got what fairly was coming to us, we would all be in trouble. We easily overestimate our own inherent goodness and performance. The good news of this story and of the Bible is that the grace of God outstrips even fairness. And the leader who remembers this power of unfair grace will be the one who breaks through ordinariness with strength and into the realm of something special.

Exercise: *Look for an opportunity to give someone today something that they could not be said to deserve. Envision and imagine how this small act of grace will be a source of infusing supernatural power and strength to you. Then ask God to show you what to do with that new strength.*

"But if you will allow me to say so, I have learned by divination that the Lord has blessed me because of you."
– Genesis 30:27

Chapter 32 ends with a woman who *"envied her sister"* (v. 1) and is full of all kinds of rivalry and deception, sometimes humorous and sometimes not. Leah out-duels her barren sister Rachel for aphrodisiac *"mandrakes"* and as a result *"hired"* her husband and conceives yet another son (vv. 14-21). Jacob cleverly tricks Laban into a deal whereby he engineers a favorable settlement for sheep and goats (vv. 31-43). Most of the story is about human maneuvering to get the upper hand over rival family members.

But in the middle is a small but critical piece of divine intrusion. Laban learns *"by divination"* that his prosperity is due to Jacob's presence. (He only figures this out by supernatural means.) Remember, Jacob is trying to dupe Laban and vice versa. But the Bible can't help itself. God has called the children of Abraham to be blessed in order to be a blessing (12:3). And so wherever Jacob goes, the people around him prosper.

In 2 Kings 13:21, even the bones of God's prophet Elisha are so powerful that to touch them accidentally causes a dead man to spring to life and stand on his feet. Many would get only close enough to Jesus to touch the *"fringe of his cloak"* and would be healed (Mark 6:56). Power leaks from these chosen people!

A leader who is called by God can remember that the power of the call and role outstrips even some of their less-than-noble behavior. Leaders called by God will even inadvertently bless others around them and cause them to experience prosperity. This is neither to excuse the leader's bad behavior nor discount the impact of the leader's decisions. But it is to say that when you are a God-called leader, you will ooze blessing to others in such a way that can only be explained supernaturally.

"This heap is a witness, and the pillar is a witness, that I will not pass beyond this heap to you, and you will not pass beyond this heap and this pillar to me, for harm."
– Genesis 31:52

Jacob, born in conflict, now sees the conflict with Laban escalate to the point where he and his abundant household flee secretly. The two men are furious with each other but have to maintain the appearance of civility. Laban is warned *"in a dream"* (v. 24) to be neutral, but even that cannot stop him from speaking impulsively (vv. 26ff).

Years of deception reach a climax when Laban accuses Jacob of stealing his *"household gods"* (v. 19), believed to insure his leadership and legitimize his property claims. Jacob didn't realize *"that Rachel had stolen the gods"* (v. 32), so the two argued again. In biting satire, the so-called "*gods*" are actually in "the red tent," sitting beneath a menstruating woman. It is the writer's wink of asking sarcastically, "Which God is God?"

The story climaxes, after yet another argument, with Jacob and Laban making a "boundary covenant" with each other. Though they can't even agree on what to call the altar (v. 48), they at least reach détente. Sometimes a truce is the best you can hope for.

Leaders who have a heart for reconciliation must sometimes understand that, in highly charged and deeply conflicted situations, détente may be the best possible outcome. Reinhold Niebuhr argued that while *love* was possible in intimate situations, the ethic of *justice* was the best one could hope for among societies or nations. We sometimes have to conclude the same. Wise leaders sometimes have to establish a boundary, agree to disagree on the specifics, go their separate ways, and call it a day.

Exercise: *Who is someone with whom a boundary covenant is the best possible outcome? Meditate today over how you might set a boundary with this person rather than wading into interminable conflict.*

"So Jacob called the place Peniel saying, "For I have seen
God face to face, and yet my life is preserved." The sun rose
upon him as he passed Penuel, limping because of his hip."
— Genesis 32:30-31

Jacob was a man who wrestled both with God and with his own demons. He was born simultaneously grabbing from his twin and yet chosen by God (25:26ff). He was close with his mother but deceived his father. His uncle's household prospered because of him but the two fought continuously. Now the time of reckoning with his twin Esau is at hand, and the best and worst of Jacob comes out.

Not knowing whether Esau will kiss him or kill him, Jacob devoutly prays to God for help and yet cowardly sends the women and children over the river first to meet his brother. He tries to bargain with both God and Esau. He divides the tribe in case he has to cut and run. All of this culminates in the famous scene where he "*wrestles*" (v. 24) with a divine being at night. Is this God? An angel? The embodiment of his own inner conflicts? Who knows?

What we do know is that he came out with a limp, and with his name changed from "*Jacob*" (grabber) to "*Israel*," his hip and thigh put out of joint and into a limp, and all of this is described as a "*blessing*" (vv. 25ff). Even the name of the place changes from "*Peniel*" to "*Penuel*." The encounter of wrestling is tied to changing, and changing is tied to moving forward both with God, the Promise, and reconciliation with his brother.

Every leader has to wrestle. Every wresting match can lead to something being "put out of joint." Every limp can lead to moving forward. The best leaders don't avoid this wrestling. They know that leading and limping are part of the same call.

Exercise: *There is someone with whom you are "out of joint," and perhaps some place with God that needs to be transformed. Are you willing to confront these and wrestle with them? If so, begin today. If not, ask God for the courage to move to that arena.*

John P. Chandler   83

Genesis 33

"But Esau said, "I have enough, my brother; keep what you have for yourself." Jacob said, "No, please; if I find favor with you, then accept my present from my hand; for truly to see your face is like seeing the face of God – since you have received me with such favor. Please accept my gift that is brought to you, because God has dealt graciously with me, and because I have everything I want." So he urged him, and he took it." – Genesis 33:9-11

Twins Jacob and Esau were deeply conflicted from the moment younger Jacob "grabbed" his elder's rightful place at birth. Having later stolen the birthright that belonged to Esau and years ago high-tailed it out of town, now comes the moment of reunion and reckoning. No wonder Jacob deeply fears retribution from his

Praying New Beginnings

brother, and sends layers of protection and waves of presents before him. Jacob limps to the encounter after having wrestled with God. And though Esau's story leading up to the encounter isn't told, it seems he has wrestled and limped, too.

But there is no showdown, no beat-down. There is no vengeful retribution.

Why not? Because Esau says, "*I have enough.*" And Jacob responds, "*I have everything I want.*" There is no more need for grabbing, deceiving, jockeying, fleeing, posturing, and fearing. Both parties know they have "*enough.*"

The apostle Paul later said, "*There is great gain in godliness combined with contentment*" (1 Timothy 6:6), and that his strength came because "*I have learned to be content with whatever I have*" (Philippians 4:11). Jacob and Esau now know that they have "*enough*" and "*everything I want.*" And with this mutuality found in contentment, the conflict can end.

When we as leaders sense the "enough-ness" of our lives, the kind of grabbing that takes what it wants at the expense of others disappears from our hearts. We can approach relationships not with a needy eye toward how we might manipulate and extract from them, but with a heart toward how we can bless the other. Gift-giving and gift-receiving now become possible. When we are able to say, "*I have enough,*" then it is possible to lead others – because it is now possible to love others out of a grateful heart.

Exercise: *Can you begin to catalogue mentally where you have "enough?" As you take inventory of all the ways in which God has provided for you, spend time expressing your gratitude.*

Genesis 34

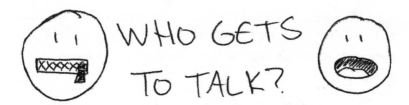

"When they heard of it, the men were indignant and very angry, because he had committed an outrage in Israel by lying with Jacob's daughter, for such a thing ought not to be done." – Genesis 34:7

Some stories are included in the Bible not to model behaviors but condemn them. This horrific story of the rape of Dinah is included because the people of God *must* discuss such odious realities and the cultural attitudes that permit them.

Dinah, daughter of Jacob, is raped by Shechem, who then wants to marry her. His father Hamor sees this as an economic and political opportunity. Her brothers, especially Simeon and Levi, are outraged at the honor offense. The men of Hamor's city are ready to cut a tribal deal with the Israelites (ironically requiring the "cut"

Praying New Beginnings

of circumcision). Only two characters involved in the whole affair never get to say a word: Dinah herself, and God.

This is why Anita Diamant's novel, *The Red Tent,* which tells the story from the voice and perspective of Dinah, is so powerful. Dinah is more than an object to be acted upon, first by rape and then repeatedly violated as a pawn of more powerful (and male) interests. And God is more than a tribal figurehead who has only symbolic interest in human affairs. Both Diamant's novel and the Bible itself stand as warnings about what happens when God and Dinah are not given a word in the story. It is interesting that the men of the story who do all of the talking pay a heavy price – Simeon and Levi are forced out of town and decline in power, and Hamor and the men of Shechem pay with their lives. Dinah certainly pays. Everyone pays.

Part of leadership is determining who gets to talk. Who gets a say in determining outcomes? Are employees affected by decisions "higher up" permitted to speak? Is the rape victim's voice silenced? Do children exploited in human trafficking get heard? Are we intentionally including female voices in traditionally boys-only discussions? If you want to lead and respond to crisis well, you better make sure to include all of the appropriate voices – including God's.

Exercise: *As you are trying to make a leadership decision, look at the situation as a story. Determine the characters in the story. Which ones get the main speaking parts? Who is acting and who is being acted upon? In what way is God determinative in the story? If needed, script an alternative plot in which all of those who need a speaking part get one, including God as the omniscient narrator of the story.*

Genesis 35-36

CLEANSING AND RENAMING

"So Jacob said to his household and to all who were with him, "Put away the foreign gods that are among you, and purify yourselves, and change your clothes; then come, let us go up to Beth-el, that I may make an altar there to the God who answered me in the day of my distress and has been with me wherever I have gone." – Genesis 35:2-3

Who knew that, at the end of the day, Jacob's sons would cause him more trouble than his brother Esau? Sons Levi and Simeon resist pagan culture violently (34:25). Reuben caves into the culture's loose sexual mores (v. 22). Neither is the way of God's people living in an alien culture.

Instead, after the awful story of the rape of Dinah and her family's completely inappropriate response, Jacob knows that his clan must change its ways. There is all kinds of renaming of people and places throughout the story. The keynote is Jacob's announcement that everyone must:

- *"put away the foreign gods that are among you";*

- *"purify yourselves";*

- *"change your clothes"* (symbolically significant as markers of new identity);

- *"then come, let us go up to Beth-el, that I may make an altar there to my God who answered me there in the day of my distress and who has been with me wherever I have gone."*

No wonder the first Christians spoke of the core ritual of cleansing and re-naming – baptism - as a matter of renouncing *"the ways you also once followed ... stripping off the old self ... (clothing) yourselves with the new selves ... and being renewed in knowledge according to the image of the creator"* (Colossians 3:7-10). In the face of our failure to live truly and well in hostile territory, we need, in Jesus' words, to *"repent and believe in the good news"* (Mark 1:15). And baptism was the ritual embracing of the change of ways and new direction.

Leaders don't always need to stand up in front of their group and announce that "we are all going to have to change our ways" and enact group symbols as the first step in that. But sometimes we do. There is a time for rituals of cleansing and renaming, and wise leaders are unafraid to call for such.

Exercise: *Is there a need to call out (vocally and publically) as unacceptable the behavior of a group you lead? If so, map out what a "purifying" ritual would look like. And as people take it on, "name" the place and time with a ritual marker that will symbolize the decisive changes made that day.*

"His brothers said to him, "Are you indeed to reign over us?
Are you indeed to have dominion over us? So they hated him
even more because of his dreams and his words."
– Genesis 37:8

The Genesis stories are about the dream of God: to bless the world with a covenant relationship, demonstrated and announced through a chosen people. The descendants of Abraham, Isaac, and

Jacob are especially blessed to reign and prosper – not because they are inherently superior (they are decidedly not!), but because they are <u>chosen</u>. God is running a beta with Israel that he wants to release on the whole world.

In the Joseph stories, this chosen-ness is demonstrated throughout by dreams. (There are three sets of two dreams each in chapters 37-50). And in the opening story here, the *"dream"* is paired with a *"robe"* (v. 3), a long colorful coat with sleeves. This robe is not for field work, but symbolizes a royal claim.

Wearing his robe and telling his dreams, Joseph is despised and ultimately sold into slavery. The robe, given in love, is torn in hate, and now used as a tool by Joseph's brothers to deceive their father. *"We shall see what will become of his dreams,"* they say sarcastically (v. 20). Christ himself would also one day be disrobed and mocked (Matthew 27:30f).

Those who lead today on behalf of the dream of God will recognize this story. We can certainly learn from Joseph's mistakes and guard against any arrogance that would rub our calling into the noses of others. But that doesn't mean we don't tell the dream and wear the robe. And the good news is, as with Joseph and later Jesus, opposition to the dream and the robe is not the last word.

Exercise: *Do people know that you are a representative for the dream of God? If so, is there a symbol of your calling? Is there something about your role as a leader and representative for God's dream that others might resent? Ask God for the humility not to flaunt it to others, and equal courage not to hide it.*

Genesis 38

"Then Judah acknowledged them and said, "She is more in the right than I, since I did not give her to my son Shelah."
– Genesis 38:26

This wild episode provides a female take on the Joseph cycle of stories in Genesis 37-50. We last saw Judah in the previous chapter, selling his brother Joseph into slavery. Now (try to keep up!), he marries, conceives three sons, marries off the first son ("*Er*") to Tamar ... sees Er slain because of wickedness ... tells the second son ("*Onan*") to "*perform the duty of a brother-in-law to her, to raise up offspring for your brother*" (v. 8) ... watches Onan be slain due to wickedness ... and finally withholds his final son ("*Shelah*") from Tamar out of fear.

And then the soap opera gets complicated! Judah inadvertently sleeps with his dressed-up-as-a-cult-prostitute daughter-in-law Tamar, who fools and then implicates him. He is ready to kill her

Praying New Beginnings

when she publically points out his sin of superstitiously avoiding his honorable duty to keep his promise and provide Shelah as her husband.

The tale is almost too bewildering to follow. But it climaxes with Judah's admission that *"she is more in the right than I,"* that his own sin was greater than Tamar's.

There is plenty of blame to spread around regarding what went wrong in this story. But any individual sexual sin (especially Tamar's prostitution) pales in comparison to the corporate or communal violations perpetrated by the men in the story on a woman like Tamar. She is used, abused, maligned, left vulnerable, and made desperate to the point of sleeping with her father-in-law just to survive. Such awful choices forced upon a person; such a terrible state of affairs!

Wise leaders pause before assigning quick blame for the sins of individuals. Yes, individuals are responsible for their own choices, and are swiftly held to account (as in the cases of Er and Onan). But often there are deeper, systemic, corporate, communal sins at work. And good leaders do the hard work of addressing these forces rather than simply pointing the quick and convenient finger of blame.

Prayer: *"Lord, make me slower to anger today at individuals I see who are failing to live well. Give me the patience to pause, reflect on the principalities and powers of wickedness at work in and around all of our lives. And grant me the courage to combat those social forces of sin rather than only blaming individual sinners. I want to live righteously both as an individual and as a community member, and ask for your help to do so. In the name of Jesus, Amen."*

RESISTANCE AND RUNNING

"*How then could I do this great wickedness and sin against God?*" – Genesis 39:9

"*The Lord was with Joseph, and he became a successful man*" (v. 2) wherever he went in Egypt. The calling is on his life, and he is working out the Dream of God. So even in a seductive and foreign place, God causes Joseph (like his father Jacob, 30:30) to prosper.

But calling and prosperity do not exempt anyone from temptation, trial, and unjust suffering. In Joseph's case, the first test is with the wife of Potiphar, who relentlessly tries to seduce him. It does not end well for Joseph. Having repeatedly spurned her advances, she cries rape. And who is going to believe the word of a poor foreigner against hers? Joseph is thrown in prison.

What is instructive is how he lives with daily temptation before everything crashes. For a long time ("*day after day*," v. 10), he actively resists and argues against her seduction. He frames it neither as a sin against her, nor his own conscience, but as a "*sin against God*." What is wrong is wrong whether you get caught or not. Eventually resistance is futile, though, and the day comes when the situation is past arguing. In that day Joseph "*fled and ran outside*" (v. 12).

We have to understand that there is a day to fight back, resist, and argue against wrongdoing. And then there comes a time is get out of the house however you can, even if you have to leave your garment behind. In this day, running doesn't mean you won't be punished, even unfairly. But while you may not keep your day job and may lose even the shirt on your back, what you will keep by running is your integrity and a clear heart before an ever-watching God. Pray that when the day comes for you to run from temptation, you will indeed run!

Exercise: *Is there a situation in your life and leadership where you are being called to stand up to evil and resist it? Or are you dallying with something to the point where the wise thing to do is to cut and run, to flee with your soul and integrity intact? Ask God for the discernment to know the difference.*

"And Joseph said to them, "Do not interpretations belong to God? Please tell them to me." – Genesis 40:8

While our culture attributes success to hard work, Joseph's story says it depends on trust in the ever-watchful care of God. His first experiences with dreams did not go so well (chapter 37). He brashly placed himself as the center of the universe, with his brothers bowing down to him. Lo and behold, it did not go over well with the brothers – imagine that!

But this time, when Joseph asks the butler and baker tell him that they both had dreams, he says, "*Do not interpretations belong to God? Tell me your dreams.*" Joseph now includes God in the center of the universe. He is making progress as his ego diminishes. For God to entrust his kingdom authority into the hands of Joseph, the Lord himself has to move more into the center of Joseph's universe. (Joseph is not completely finished growing in humility, which is probably why he languishes for two years in prison, overlooked by an ungrateful butler who forgot about him the moment he was set free.)

Hopefully we don't have to go to prison to learn the invaluable lesson that all gifts originate with God. Ego can be a powerful inhibiter to leadership, and Joseph grows as a leader when he begins to attribute his gifts of dream discernment to the work of the Almighty.

My friends in twelve-step recovery have told me that "Ego" stands for "Ease God Out." Pride can do that to leaders; it can overshadow even remarkable gifts. These same friends say that the remedy toward wellness is to "strive for progress, not perfection." We are never done in our battle with pride, are we? But the trajectory of Joseph's journey from kidnapping, false accusation, and false imprisonment to a place where he rules the Middle East marches through his battle with ego. As he begins to replace hubris with humility, the Lord begins to use him.

And God can use our leadership as we do the same.

Exercise: *Where is ego an issue for you? Is hardship required to root it out of your life and leadership? In what way today can you begin (like Joseph) to attribute whatever you have to offer to others as a gift from God and not a function of your own brilliance?*

Genesis 41

FOR THE BENEFIT OF OTHERS

"So Pharaoh said to Joseph, "Since God has shown you all this, there is no one so discerning and wise as you. You shall be over my house, and all my people shall order themselves as you command ....." **– Genesis 41:39-40**

My friend, psychiatrist Lance Foster, says that our dreams can be the result of "day residue, a full bladder, or revelation from God." Joseph's life-experience of unexpected favor followed by undeserved hardship helps him to understand the king of Egypt's weird dreams (fat/skinny cows, good/blighted ears of corn). The key to this story is that, finally, Joseph has dealt with his ego: *"Joseph answered Pharaoh, "It is not I; God will give Pharaoh a favorable answer"* (v. 16). No longer is Joseph in it for his own enlargement. He views himself as a vehicle in the hand of the Most High God for wisdom which will serve a nation and the greater Dream of God.

Now God is able to use Joseph as his representative to rule! Joseph becomes the wise interpreting agent of dreams for the benefit of others. And as he acknowledges God as his source and himself as God's vehicle, he is entrusted with correspondingly great responsibility. *"All the world came to Joseph in Egypt to buy grain ..."* (v. 57).

In many instances in the Old Testament, God chooses to speak directly to his followers (Abraham, Moses). Sometimes God speaks indirectly, through the mouths of others (as through the prophet Nathan to David). In Joseph's story, God speaks through dreams. They are not evident to everyone and require interpretation. The function of leadership in these stories is that of *interpreting the dream for the benefit of others*. Joseph's life stumbles when his gift of leadership/wisdom/interpretation is for his own elevation. But later, he is entrusted with much by using his leadership gift and opportunity for the benefit of others.

God is the real actor in this story – not Pharaoh, and not Joseph. The moment Joseph realizes this, he is entrusted with leadership. Leadership always follows this sort of humility. True leaders acknowledge God as the source of the Dream, and themselves as stewards of that Dream and servants of others.

Exercise: *Has God given you a unique gift and a unique opportunity to influence others? If so, begin the day by openly acknowledging God as the source of that gift and opportunity. Ask for a humble spirit that credits God when you are praised. And at least one time today, consciously make a leadership decision that will benefit others and not yourself. At the end of the day, review your action and pray to be given divine wisdom to know how to interpret it.*

Genesis 42

FAILURE TO FORGIVE

"When Joseph saw his brothers, he recognized them, but he treated them like strangers and spoke harshly to them."
– Genesis 42:7

Walter Brueggemann, in his sermon, "*A Fourth-Generation Sellout*," wonders why the God of the Bible is referred to as the "*God of Abraham, Isaac, and Jacob*" – but doesn't include Joseph. *"The guy in the fourth generation of Israel's memory drops out of the mantra."* (*The Collected Sermons of Walter Brueggemann*, p. 164). Genesis 12-50 is the story about these four; but only three make the motto.

Brueggemann argues that Joseph is omitted because he sold out the Dream of God for prosperity as a chaplain and manager in imperial Egypt. I would suggest another angle. I think Joseph is not remembered in the same way because he does not early enough wield his power for honest confrontation and powerful forgiveness.

Chapter 42 is the beginning of a long back-and-forth story where powerful Joseph recognizes his famine-driven brothers who long ago sold him down the river. But rather than confront them directly and openly, Joseph toys with them for years. He sends them back and forth from Israel to Egypt, putting money in their sacks, imprisoning them randomly, playing with the whole family's emotions and futures. He has no moral qualms about doing so. Ultimately, he comes clean, all is revealed, and the family is more-or-less reconciled. But not before Joseph tortures those who once tortured him.

The first power given to those like Joseph is the power to *forgive*. If, when you are granted leadership, you do not learn to temper your power with grace, you will only further cycles of betrayal, chaos, famine, and anguish. You will never have authority unless you learn to wield power. And the first power available to Joseph – and to you – is the power to forgive. As Mike Breen says, *"If we can't handle that power to forgive, then we certainly won't be able to represent God in other ways."* Joseph eventually gets there. But not before making others pay.

Forgiveness is never easy – especially when it pertains to our family members. But when we have power in our hands through virtue of our leadership role, failing to forgive is costly for everyone involved.

Exercise: *Is there someone in your life – especially within your family – whom you need to forgive? Perhaps it is a matter for you to settle in your heart, or perhaps it needs to be a very direct verbal confrontation where you name the wrong and choose to forgive it. Ask for God to give you the grace and the will to forgive <u>early</u> in your leadership rather than late.*

Genesis 43

"Now the men were afraid because they were brought to
Joseph's house, and they said, "It is because of the money,
replaced in our sacks the first time, that we have an
opportunity to fall upon us, to make slaves of us and take
our donkeys." – Genesis 43:18

Praying New Beginnings

One of the great themes of this chapter is the ability to give and receive generosity and hospitality. Jacob, just as he had done earlier in his life with brother Esau (32:20), sends a very nice present (*"choice fruits of the land,"* v. 11) ahead to Joseph in advance of the brothers meeting him. He also sends *"double the money"* and his prized remaining son, the youngest *"Benjamin"* (v. 15).

Joseph responds with hospitality, instructing his *"steward"* to prepare a feast (v. 16). But where Joseph is presumably able to receive the gifts brought to him, the brothers are never able to enjoy fully the feast prepared for them. They are *"afraid"* and wonder if they are being set up to be imprisoned as *"slaves"* (v. 18)!

Certainly Joseph's brothers are wary because they are at the mercy of a powerful man. But it is striking that a feast is given by a prince in their honor, they who are needy receive a reception fit for royalty – and their primary reaction is fear and worry. *"The men were afraid"* because they were full of guilt about their betrayal of many years ago.

When beset with guilt and fear, we are unable not only to offer generosity and hospitality, but we are also unable to receive it. A feast can be set before us – and we will worry if we are being set up. Self-leadership involves clearing the deck of un-reconciled relationships that wrack us with guilt for what we have done and fear of what others will do to us. Such reconciliation has to occur for there to be human exchanges of hospitality and generosity.

Exercise: *Is there a relationship in your life – even in the distant past – with which you need to make peace in order to fully experience the hospitality and generosity of others (and of God)? If so, begin to pray today for God to give you the wisdom of how to respond.*

Genesis 44

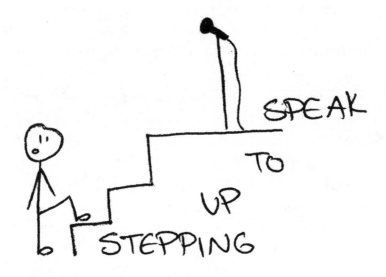

"Then Judah stepped up to him and said, "O my lord, let your servant please speak a word in my lord's ears, and do not be angry with your servant ...." – Genesis 44:18

This chapter lacks for nobility. The sins of Joseph's brothers are finding them out. Jacob's selfish spoiling of Benjamin, his youngest son, is proving to a snare to the whole family. And Joseph is using his power to deceive, manipulate, and dangle his family over a pit. God is mentioned in the story only once (v. 16), as the one who finds out *"guilt."*

Yet God is not absent from this story. The divine presence is found in Judah's moving speech to his brother, where he pleads for

Joseph to accept his life as a substitute for imprisoned Benjamin. It is a brave speech, full of confession, honesty, and (finally!) self-giving and sacrificial love. What is the outcome of the speech? *"Then Joseph could no longer control himself before all those who stood before him, and he cried out, "Send everyone away from me"* (45:1). Joseph is moved to the point of revelation. He confesses the providence of God, comes clean with his brothers, and hastens the process of reconciliation and family provision.

It all began when Judah *"stepped up"* to speak. It is not his first speech. Judah earlier convinced his brothers not to kill Joseph but instead sell him into slavery (37:26). He also gave a public speech acknowledging his *mea culpa* in the affair with Tamar (38:26). Each instance of Judah's stepping up to speak is a game-changer.

There are plenty of biblical admonitions for us to be people of action and not merely of words. But there is a time and place for a leader to step up into a spiraling situation and make a game-changing speech. These speeches are full of humility and confession of sin, brutal honesty, self-giving sacrifice, and acknowledgment of our powerlessness to control. In this sense they are like prayers. When the situation is desperate and the time is right, leaders step up to speak.

Exercise: *Is there a speech you need to "step up" to make? If so, what is the content of that speech and who is the audience? For what will you ask boldly? When is the time to make that difficult speech? Meditate upon this speech. Ask God to give you the resolve to speak out loud and not merely internally. Confess your resolve to speak to a friend who will hold you accountable to follow through. And watch for the providence of God!*

Genesis 45

GOD SENT ME

"God sent me before you to preserve life."

"God sent me before you to preserve a remnant on earth ..."

"So it was not you who sent me here, but God ..."
– Genesis 45:5, 7, 8

While the stories of Abraham, Isaac, and Jacob were rural and nomadic and focused on the Promise of God, the story of Joseph is very urban and about living with wisdom as a minority under foreign rule. Such wisdom is gained by profound <u>remembering</u> (of the Promise or Dream of God) and <u>forgetting</u> (of grievous and sinful

Praying New Beginnings

wrongs perpetrated). The art of wisdom in the city is the knowing how and what to remember and forget.

The key phrase of chapter 45 – mentioned three times (vv. 5, 7, 8) – is *"**God** sent me."* The brothers didn't ultimately send Joseph. He didn't ultimately choose and claw his own way to the top. His prominence and the reconciliation depends ultimately on the providence (literally *pro-video*, "to see before") of God to work in all things for God. As Walter Brueggemann puts it, beyond the guilt of the brothers, grief of father Jacob, and revenge of Joseph lies the hidden and providential work of God, "in, with, and under human actions." Ultimately, there is salvation for Joseph's whole family because of the God-sent nature beneath every twist and turn of events. As it turns out, God is involved in lots more than any of them realized. Joseph and his family are finally characters in another story, another Dream, much larger than themselves.

An ego can be a dangerous thing for a leader, especially when it forgets that s/he is first and most an actor in another Dream and not primarily the producer of their own story. To acknowledge with humility the God-sent nature of my life and leadership is the first step toward proper remembering, proper forgetting, and ultimately to wise life in the city.

Exercise: *Where is humility a challenge for you? In the quiet of your own heart, ask God to give you a humility that allows for proper remembering of providence, proper forgetting of grievances done by others to you, and wise navigation of the challenges as a bearer of God's dream in a community governed by something other than that. Look for an opportunity today to temper whatever control or power you have with the humility that comes from being "God-sent."*

Genesis 46

"I myself will go down with you to Egypt, and I will also bring you up again; and Joseph's own hand shall close your eyes."
— Genesis 46:4

The transformation of Joseph is that the hatefulness of his brothers and his own capacity for revenge has been turned in the direction of mercy, reconciliation, and provision amidst famine. Now his father Jacob resolves to leave his country at the end of his life to see his long-lost son. Jacob *"offered sacrifices"* in worship (v. 2) and in response, God speaks to him *"in visions of the night"* (v. 3). In the vision, God reaffirms the Promise first made to forebear Abraham in

Praying New Beginnings

12:3, declares that the Promise will still be valid in a foreign land, and tells Jacob *"do not be afraid."* This is followed by a lengthy genealogy, which affirms that this is much more than a private matter between Jacob and God; this is about God's work with his whole people.

And there you have it: there is more going on in the stories of Jacob, Joseph, and the family than meets the eye. The hidden purposes of God for his people – and indeed for the whole world – are at work here. God is not localized in Canaan only but *"will go down with you to Egypt"* (and *"up again"*). God travels! This is not "fate" or "destiny" or the "stars aligning" in "luck." It is something much deeper than that. As Walter Brueggemann says, "God takes initiatives for our lives which may run counter to our own best intentions. Faithful people pay attention to this hiddenness, and are willingly led by it." Jacob was. Joseph was. Jesus was.

A leader's personal story is important to his or her leadership. But God has a story, too. It is larger than any individual's story. And any individual who would lead in a holy manner will quickly acknowledge the larger and sometimes hidden story as the context in which s/he leads.

This is how God became more than local for Jacob. It is how Joseph broke destructive family cycles and brought reconciliation. It is how God worked for the nation Israel even through its period of enslavement. And it is how our smaller and sometimes confusing stories are caught up in purposes much greater and larger.

Prayer: *"Lord, grant to me today a confident sense of the grand size of your story. I ask for the faith to trust in your hidden, good work. Give my soul a sense of being carried along in the great river of your love, in the name of Jesus our Lord, Amen."*

John P. Chandler

JACOB BLESSED PHAROAH

"Then Joseph brought in his father Jacob, and presented him before Pharaoh, and Jacob blessed Pharaoh." – Genesis 47:7

Dark shadows are appearing in the story. Jacob summarizes his years as *"few and hard"* (v. 9). Joseph executes a royal program that results in the short-term feeding but long-term enslaving of his own people. Even on his deathbed, Jacob says, *"Do not bury me in*

Egypt" (v. 29), knowing that life in even the best of Egypt is not the fulfillment of the Promise of God. We remember that the context of this story is a great famine in the land. In a few short chapters, a Pharaoh *"who did not know Joseph"* (Exodus 1:8) will rise to power, and things will turn nasty.

Yet in the middle of these troubling signals, a remarkable thing happens in the encounter of the most powerful person in Egypt and a seemingly-needy and dependent bearer of God's Promise, Jacob. Pharaoh doesn't bless Jacob; Jacob blesses Pharaoh. Jacob wishes for the ruler of the land welfare and long life. And indeed, that thriving came to pass for the Pharaoh. In so doing, Jacob is fulfilling God's command to Abraham in Genesis 12:3: that God's people would not only be *"blessed"* but that *"in you all the families of the earth shall be blessed."*

This work of Jacob to bless Pharaoh foreshadows the teaching of Jesus, who said, *"Love your enemies, do good to those who hate you, bless those who curse you, pray for those who abuse you"* (Luke 6:27f). The God-called life is greater than a simple equation. God-called people are not simple recipients of divine advantages. We actually parlay those blessings onto people who don't seem to deserve them.

There is much talk of "accountability" in leadership today. But if a leader cannot also learn to pass on undeserved grace, their life and leadership will become small, cold, and calculated.

Exercise: *As a practice, can you think of a way to pass along undeserved blessing and affirmation to someone today? Ask God to give you a perspective beyond the immediate "unfairness" of this, and into the longer-term realm of living by grace and not law.*

John P. Chandler

Genesis 48

THREE DIMENSIONS OF BLESSING

"(Jacob) blessed Joseph, and said, "The God before whom my ancestors walked, the God who has been my shepherd all my life to this day, the angel who has redeemed me from all harm, bless the boys; and in them let my name be perpetuated, and the name of my ancestors Abraham and Isaac; and let them grow into a multitude on the earth." – Genesis 48:15-16

This is a deathbed story, intended to show that life's final transitions are for blessing. It shows us how to bless deeply. The brackets of the story are father Jacob's touching <u>adoption</u> of Joseph's foreign-born sons (vv. 1-7), and a <u>reversal</u> (vv. 8ff) bestowing extra grace not on first-born *"Manasseh"* but younger grandson *"Ephraim,"* echoing Jacob's own experience of being chosen over his older twin Esau (Genesis 27). The reversal and adoption demonstrate that blessings are to include radically and bestow graciously.

The content of the blessing is a three-fold description of the nature of God. It assumes that the font of all blessing from one generation to the next flows out of the very action of God to us. Jacob asks that God be experienced in his grandsons as the:

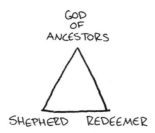

GOD
OF
ANCESTORS

SHEPHERD   REDEEMER

- *"The God before whom my ancestors Abraham and Isaac walked"* – this God is eternal, consistent, steady, reliable, and the Lord of a meta-narrative, Promise, and Dream greater than any single human story;
- *"the God who has been my shepherd to this day"* – a blessing that they experience God as a care-giving, nourishment-providing guide (Psalm 23) who does not abandon in the day of death but is faithful to the end; and
- *"the angel who has redeemed me from all harm"* – Jacob hopes for the next generation to experience the God who rescues, protects, and delivers. The image of *"redeemed"* also connotes a slave or hostage whose freedom has been bought by another.

This is so much richer than an inheritance of, "You can divide up my stuff!" It longs for the next generation to experience God as faithful companion, feeding guide, and strong deliverer.

Such blessing which passes along the worthy experience of God is not only for grandfathers to grandsons, but also the role of leaders who are passing the mantle. We have our example: we are wish for those who are to live and lead behind us the full riches of the God who has been the God of our ancestors, our shepherd and redeemer.

Exercise: *To whom will you need to pass on a blessing? What will be the content of that blessing? How will the blessing reflect your testimony of having experienced God? When and how will you do this?*

Genesis 49

THE STORY OF YOUR LIFE

"The Jacob called his sons, and said, "Gather around, that I may tell you what will happen to you in days to come."
– Genesis 49:1

Jacob's final act was to gather his family and render a poem that both summarizes and forecasts their lives. The speech also functions to summarize the movement of the book of Genesis, and to sketch the contours of the waxing and waning of various Israelite tribes over many centuries.

The speech combines aphorisms, metaphors, and oracles. It is not sugary but a clear-eyed and at times brutally honest series of pronouncements. It summarizes who persons (and tribes) have become because of their life choices, and forecasts their future story based on those summaries.

From a leadership perspective, what is fascinating here is how one or two verses can sum up a person's life in a way that is powerful and determinative. Obviously, in twenty words, it is impossible to capture the complexity of any individual's story. But while it doesn't mean everything, it does mean something. Each *"blessing"* (v. 28) marks and characterizes a trajectory into which the person who receives it lives into. It shapes them and frames the story of their life.

So a leader must ask, "How am I telling the story about myself and the people around me? What is the one-verse summary of my life that both gathers the story so far, and shapes the story to come?" A blessing or curse is a powerful thing. Every leader will be intentional in pronouncing it.

Exercise: *Ask, "What is the one-verse story of my life so far?" If you haven't already done so, write one. And pick another person that you lead or need to bless, and do the same for him or her.*

Genesis 50

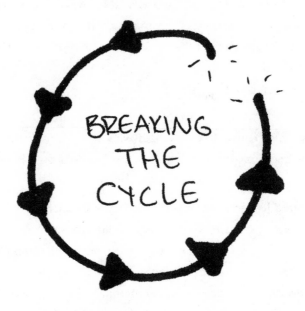

"But Joseph said to them, "Do not be afraid! Am I in the place of God? Even though you intended to do harm to me, God intended it for good, as he is doing today. So have no fear; I will provide for you and your little ones." In this way he reassured them, speaking kindly to them."
– Genesis 50:19-21

When Joseph reassures his fearful brothers that while they meant for evil, *"God intended it for good,"* his sentence stands alongside of the great biblical pronouncements of reconciliation amidst wreckage, hope in the middle of havoc:

- The prophet Jeremiah assuring the exiles in Babylon, *"For surely I know the plans I have for you, says the Lord, plans for your welfare and not for harm, to give you a future with hope"* (Jeremiah 29:11);

Praying New Beginnings

- Paul reminding the suffering church, *"We know that all things work together for good for those who love God, who are called according to his purpose"* (Romans 8:28); and

- Jesus' story of the loving father's response to the resentful older brother about the return of the groveling prodigal son: *"But we had to celebrate and rejoice, because this brother of yours was dead and has come to life; he was lost and has been found"* (Luke 15:32).

So when Joseph breaks decades or even generations of revenge with a pronouncement of forgiveness, he is doing more than his daily kind deed. He is enacting the very heart of the story of the Bible: that the purposes of God trump human bitterness and make possible a new way of community beyond old resentments.

It is Joseph's crowning achievement and final act. It is greater than his ability to survive hardship; greater than his ability to interpret dreams; and greater than his stunning rise to power in his family and over the whole land. Joseph's pinnacle is when he chooses forgiveness over fighting and reconciliation over revenge.

When the window of opportunity opens for a leader to make the determinative speech of his or her life, what speech will it be? Will the leader exercise dominance, power, and control? Or will s/he break old and bad cycles, show radical kindness, and forgive in a way that makes way for new possibilities with God and people?

Exercise: *Do you have your speech ready for what you will say when the moment of truth comes and you are able to have the critical conversation with someone who has wronged you and when you have the upper hand? What will you say in that speech? Will it be to tell them off, curse them, or pronounce forgiveness and a new way? Rehearse in your mind (and perhaps on paper) the speech you would make in that moment.*

John P. Chandler

Exodus 1

"But the midwives feared God; they did not do as the king of Egypt commanded them." – Exodus 1:17

The last word in the book of Genesis is *"Egypt"* – always code for "slavery." So the people of God have traveled from:

Eden Garden paradise → Egyptian "(oppression) with forced labor" (v. 11)

Promise of Land → "(building) supply cities" for "taskmasters" (v. 11)

Promise of heirs (Isaac, Jacob, Joseph) → genocide of their infants (v. 16)

Praying New Beginnings

How they fell into this state of Egyptian slavery is the story of Genesis and the story of sin. How they are going to get out is the story of Exodus.

And while Exodus will later center around Moses as a deliverer, the overture of its first two chapters is that deliverance was triggered by the faithfulness of five women, including *"Hebrew midwives … named Shiprah and Puah"* (v. 15). The supposedly powerful *"Pharaoh"* is never named, but the midwives who have real power are! They are named and remembered in history because of their faithful obedience in hard situations. *"Because the midwives feared God, he gave them families"* (v. 21).

This is a corrective for leaders whose egos get far enough out of check to start believing their own press. The outcomes of nations, companies, peoples, and movements don't finally rest on the celebrities in charge. Those outcomes rest on the faithfulness of ordinary people like *"Shiprah and Puah"* who disobey an unjust king in order to obey the true God. Faithfulness from ordinary people leads to Exodus out of Egypt, and forward toward new Eden.

Exercise: *If there is an organizational chart of those you lead, print a copy. (If you are thinking about your leadership in a family or something that doesn't have an official chart, sketch out a simple one with the lead decision-maker on the top of the chart.) Now turn the paper upside down. Pray for the faithful obedience to God of those ordinary folk now at the top. And remember them as you lead.*

Exodus 2

FIVE ORDINARY DIFFERENCE MAKERS

"When the child grew up, she brought him to Pharaoh's daughter, and she took him as her son. She named him Moses, "because," she said, "I drew him out of the water."
– Exodus 2:10

Scholar Walter Brueggemann notes that the grand movement of Exodus is from:

Slavery → Worship

Bondage → Bonding with God

Enforced Construction → Glad building of the tabernacle

Sin and the Flood (Genesis) → Delivery through the water (Exodus)

The first two chapters of Exodus give the clue as to how that grand movement was triggered through five women: *"Shiprah and Puah"* (1:13ff), the *"Levite woman"* who bore Moses (2:1ff), the *"daughter of Pharaoh"* (vv. 5ff) who defied her father and saved Moses from death, and Moses' *"sister"* Miriam (vv. 6ff) who courageously arranged for Moses' mother to nurse him.

The name *"Moses"* means *"I drew him out of the water."* This foreshadows how God will later deliver his people through the Red Sea. (As baptism signifies, it also indicates how God is always faithful to deliver his people from death and chaos.) But lest we mistakenly believe that salvation came because of charismatic Moses, Exodus 2 reminds us that Moses was an impulsive murderer (vv. 11ff). And were it not for the faithfulness of five ordinary people (*"women"* at that!), Moses never would have made it out of the waters of the Nile River in the first place. You never get to cross the Red Sea later unless you get out of the Nile first.

Leaders would do well to remember that their current platform would not exist were it not for the courage, risk, cleverness, and faithfulness of many ordinary people. These ordinary folk seldom make headlines. But they are the first stories of the Bible when explaining the origins of deliverance. A good leader never forgets that.

Exercise: *Write down the names of five people whose faithfulness to God has formed you as a person and a leader. Pause to give thanks, by name, of each of these five. Praise God for putting them in front of your life. Give thanks to God for something specific about each one.*

John P. Chandler 121

Exodus 3

BEYOND INSTINCTS
AND IMPULSES

"Then the Lord said, "I have observed the misery of my people who are in Egypt; I have heard their cry on account of their taskmasters. Indeed, I know of their sufferings, and I have come down to deliver them from the Egyptians, and to bring them up out of that land to a good and broad land, a land flowing with milk and honey ...." – Exodus 3:7-8

The call of Moses to lead is a call for him to join God in defending the weak. But while Moses has some instincts for this calling, he is a work in progress.

First, Moses tries to defend the weak by murdering an Egyptian who is *"beating a Hebrew"* (2:11). Moses' first attempt at leadership fails, because his instinct for justice is expressed impulsively and by taking matters into his own hands. Then, Moses defends the weak by driving away shepherds who were preventing women from watering their flocks (2:17). At least he doesn't kill anyone this time, so that's an improvement!

Finally, the time is right for Moses to act because God has set things in motion. No longer a vigilante, Moses joins God in the deliverance God is triggering (2:24f, 3:7ff, 3:16ff). He stops to *"turn aside"* to the burning bush he encounters (3:2). Like that bush, Moses himself has been *"blazing"* but *"not consumed"* (3:2). He has been singed but is not toast; he has discovered some things about how (and how not) to lead. God can now use Moses to defend the weak because has learned how to respond to *God's* call and timing rather than impulsively forcing the issue.

Becoming a leader is a process. No one flips a switch and suddenly makes Moses a great leader. He grows through fits and starts, making mistakes that were both costly and ultimately redemptive. But leadership requires more than instincts and impulses. It requires honing beyond impulsivity until the leader is ready to join the God who ultimately defends the weak.

Exercise: *Name one or two early mistakes you made as a leader. What did these mistakes teach you about the dangers of leading on "gut feelings?" Reflect on the dangers of when you lead solely by instinct, and pray for your own patience in waiting on revelation from God.*

THE COSTS OF
RESISTANCE
AND
HESITATION

"Then Moses answered, "But suppose they do not believe me or listen to me, but say, "The Lord did not appear to you." The Lord said to him, "What is that in your hand?" He said, "A staff." – Exodus 4:1-2

When God appears to Moses with a burning-bush commission to lead, Moses responds with haggling and foot-dragging. Specifically, he asks God,

1. *"Who am I"* for the job? (3:11)

2. Who are <u>you</u> to send me? (3:13ff)

3. *"Suppose they do not believe me or listen to me?"* (4:1)

4. *"I have never been eloquent"* (4:10).

We know that these are not the eager, legitimate questions of someone who wants to be thoroughly faithful, but are, essentially, dodges – because after exhausting every possible excuse, Moses finally flat-out says to God, *"please send someone else"* (v. 13). And *"the anger of the Lord was kindled against Moses"* (v. 14).

God was angry because he would never have commissioned Moses unless he had also equipped him for the job. When God asked Moses, *"What is that in your hand?"* and Moses showed him the staff that would become the first sign, God was telling Moses that he had everything he needed to do the work. But while God had faith in Moses, Moses had little faith in God, or in himself.

As a result of this reluctance and cowardice, God concedes to pair Moses with *"your brother Aaron ... he can speak fluently"* (v.14). While Aaron gives some temporary help, he will be a spiritual impediment to Moses' and God's work later (see Exodus 32).

There are great and grave costs to resistance and hesitation. Henry Blackaby says, "When God speaks to you, what you do next reveals what you believe about God." When we drag our feet reluctantly (sometimes in the name of carefulness), our procrastination exacts real and ongoing costs. If Exodus 2 shows the costs of impulsivity, then Exodus 3-4 shows the costs of resistance and hesitation.

Exercise: *Reflect on a time when dragging your feet in a leadership task has been costly to you and others. Is there any area of procrastination or excuse-making going on in your life now? If so, don't waste any more time reflecting on it – resolve to address it today!*

Exodus 5

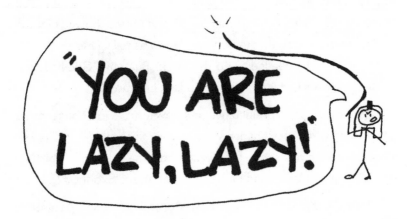

"He said, "You are lazy, lazy; that is why you say, "Let us go and sacrifice to the Lord." – Exodus 5:17

Moses' life has already journeyed from palace to pasture, and now he returns to the palace of the Egyptian Pharaoh. But what was once a "home game" is now an "away game." All Moses has is his call from God, his *"Thus says the Lord ..."* (v. 1). Fourth-century bishop

Praying New Beginnings

Gregory of Nyssa wrote that like Moses, "We regard falling from God's friendship as the only thing dreadful and we consider becoming God's friend the only thing worthy of honor and desire. This, as I have said, is the perfection of life."

However, having seen a burning bush doesn't get him very far with the Pharaoh. It's no accident that the architecture of Egypt is a pyramid, and Pharaoh was the top point. He saw no room for competitors.

So when Moses appeals to release the people to "celebrate a festival" (v. 1) to God, the king of Egypt does not do the happy dance. He calls the people, "lazy, lazy" (vv. 8, 17). He demands that they make bricks without straw. And he has Israelite "supervisors" and Egyptian "taskmasters" beat the people (v. 14). Now, everyone is furious with Moses – "you have brought us into a bad odor with Pharaoh" (v. 21) – and Moses wonders what kind of mess God has gotten him into (vv. 22f).

A spiritual leader must understand that simply declaring their clear sense of God's calling is no guarantee of easy sailing. In fact, you may just as likely be regarded by the boss as lazy and your peers as a trouble-maker. Just saying "Thus says the Lord" doesn't make you a leader. Doubling down on your friendship with God in the midst of opposition <u>does</u>.

Prayer: "O Lord, if I face opposition today – if people malign and mistrust me as I speak of what you have called – let me not take my cues from them but from you. Let me find my identity in your friendship and calling and not in the approval of others. In the name of Jesus, who did this, Amen."

Exodus 6

WHY PEOPLE DON'T LISTEN

"Moses told this to the Israelites; but they would not listen to Moses because of their broken spirit and their cruel slavery."
– Exodus 6:9

Moses lacks confidence in his speaking, and the Pharaoh has no intentions of releasing his free labor force. But we also learn that the Israelites *"would not listen"* and would not cooperate with those who would free them. Their exhaustion and oppression is to blame: *"because of their broken spirit* (their internal condition) *and cruel slavery"* (their context and circumstances). The Israelites did not have the ability to hear what God and Moses came to say.

Fred Craddock revolutionized preaching in North America when he voiced the insight that great preaching is not simply a matter of what comes out of the mouth of the preacher. Great preaching happens *in the ear of the hearer.* The communication circuit is not closed until the "what I said" of the preacher is received with the "what you heard" of the listener. Your eloquence matters not if my ear garbles your words.

Sometimes people don't go where leaders want to take them because the people are not able to listen. Moses would retrospectively explain the situation before he died by saying that God had not *"given you a mind to understand, or eyes to see, or ears to hear"* (Deuteronomy 29:4).

When this is the state of the listeners, a great leader doesn't polish the speech. S/he instead explores the circumstances preventing people from hearing. Perhaps listeners are battered, worn down, or hopeless. If so, a great leader will begin to address those chronic conditions until the listener is in a position to hear. Only then is it time for that great speech.

Exercise: *Is there someone who is not listening to you? Step back from your irritation or frustration with this, and contemplate the question of* <u>why</u> *they are not listening. Is there some fear, brokenness, or situation that is blocking their receptivity? Pray about their circumstances and ask God to address the things in their world that contribute to their non-listening.*

Exodus 7

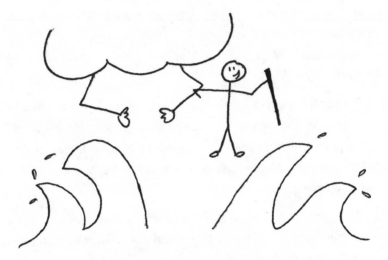

COOPERATING WITH GOD

"The Lord said to Moses, "Say to Aaron, "Take your staff and stretch out your hand over the waters of Egypt – over its rivers, its canals, and its ponds – so that they may become blood; and there shall be blood throughout the whole land of Egypt...." – Exodus 7:19

Praying New Beginnings

The time for Moses' self-doubt has passed. So has the time for verbal negotiations with a clearly hard-hearted Pharaoh (v. 3). Even the warning shot of turning Moses' staff into a snake fails to impress (v. 10). Now is the time for action.

Ancient rabbis said the plagues corresponded to Egyptian crimes against the Israelites. Origen described them as deviations from the divine law, foreshadowing the Ten Commandments. What is clear is that God, through Moses, is speaking truth to power at the very heart of Egyptian identity and rule – by corrupting the Nile, which was source of its economy, and turning its water into blood. How did this happen? By divine collaboration between God's command and power, and Moses' action to *"stretch out your hand over the waters of Egypt."*

And so every act of God-infused spiritual leadership since that day has gone. It is a sacramental combination of God's miraculous power at work, yet done in conjunction with the action of a human leader appointed to voice and enact the task. The Nile turns to blood in the meeting of God's command and Moses' staff.

Remember that it takes *both*. God typically chooses to do his works of power in the world through human agency. And we who are responding to divine call should also always remember that we are not on assignment through our own power alone.

Meditation: *Which are you more likely to neglect – the reality that when God is at work, power is at hand? Or that God wants to enact some of those things using what is in <u>your</u> hand?*

John P. Chandler   131

THE COSTS OF STUBBORNNESS

"And the magicians said to Pharaoh, "This is the finger of God!" But Pharaoh's heart was hardened, and he would not listen to them." – Exodus 8:19

The fight is on. The ten plagues correspond to and symbolize God's power as greater than that of the Egyptian gods. The Egyptian protector god Amanuet cannot protect, and their savior god Anhur cannot save. Their sun god Ra will be blotted out and their earth god Geb is helpless to prevent creation from going awry. To highlight that the God of Israel is Lord of lords, Moses not only speaks the plagues into being, but prays them into ceasing (vv. 12f).

The remarkable contrast in the story is between how Egyptians respond. Amazingly, the magicians of Egypt – the direct competitors to Moses (7:11, 22) – confess the superiority of Israel's God: *"This is the finger of God!"* These are the last people you would expect to confess faith, and the last words you would expect from enemies of the God of the Bible.

On the other hand, Pharaoh *"hardened his heart"* and *"would not listen"* or *"let them go"* (vv. 15, 19, 32). He would do so many more times. At this point, the plagues are impressive, but merely nuisances to Egypt. It appears that they must become more lethal before Pharaoh is willing to listen. He will only learn the hard way.

A bad leader is a stubborn non-listener. Stubbornness is not somehow an indicator of one's strength of convictions. It is a refusal to learn the easy way, a "hardening of the heart" that refuses to engage the evidence. Think of how much easier it would have been for Egypt had Pharaoh listened to Moses early on! Stubbornness in leadership exacts huge costs.

Exercise: *Reflect on your own "stubbornness index." How much does it take for you to change your mind? To whom to you listen in negotiations? Can you learn the easy way? What are the costs to yourself and those you lead of any stubbornness in your life?*

Exodus 9

*"But this is why I have let you live: to show you my power,
and to make my name resound through all the earth."*
– Exodus 9:16

Pharaoh's repeatedly stubborn and hard-hearted refusal to listen to God through the voice of Moses cannot be easily explained. In some places, Exodus says he persistently chose not to listen: *"he sinned once more and hardened his heart"* (v. 34). In others places, the story says that *"the Lord hardened the heart of Pharaoh, and he would not listen to them, just as the Lord had spoken to Moses"* (v. 12). Who did the hardening? The story is content to let both explanations sit side-by-side. After all, then and now, it is truly a mystery why people don't listen and learn after repeated experiences.

What is clearly demonstrated in the story, though, is the cost of the leader's non-listening. Certainly there were personal costs to Pharaoh. He had to admit publicly that *"I and my people are in the wrong"* (v. 27), losing face. Later, his own firstborn son would die because of his hard-heartedness (12:29).

But in chapter 9, the focus is on the environmental and even cosmic repercussions of Pharaoh's poor listening and leadership. The *"pestilence"* is a direct result (v. 15) and shows whose *"name"* and *"power"* rule. Pharaoh's problem is pride: *"You are still exalting yourself against my people"* (v. 17). Because of that pride, the fury of heaven is unleashed: thunder and lightning, hail and rain. Most of the first plagues (frogs, gnats, and flies) were warning shots, pesky but not lethal. The stakes are now higher, even cosmic. Crops are ruined, anthrax unleashed, the earth and skies on fire.

When we lead, we have a platform for making God's *"name resound through all the earth."* But when in pride and stubbornness we choose to do otherwise, the consequences are not just a nuisance. They exact environmental and cosmic costs.

Prayer: *"Lord of all creation, in whatever role I lead today, help me to listen well, humble myself, and serve as a steward of your reputation and name. Make me mindful of the ripple effects from my open posture to you, and careful not to close my ears or heart to your direction. Remind me of the environmental and cultural impact of my choices today. In the name of Jesus, Amen."*

DEVOLVED INTO DARKNESS

"So Moses stretched out his hand toward heaven, and there was dense darkness in all of the land of Egypt for three days. People could not see one another, and for three days they could not move from where they were; but all the Israelites had light where they lived." – Exodus 10:22-23

Praying New Beginnings

The plagues of locusts and darkness form a story of anti-creation. The *"wind"* which once swept over the formless void in Genesis 1:2 now sweeps destroying locusts into Egypt (vv. 12ff), creation regressing back toward a state of chaos. The God who said *"Let there be light"* (Genesis 1:3) now says speaks a paralyzing and immobilizing *"darkness that can be felt"* (v. 21) over the land – a darkness that mirrors that within Pharaoh's hard heart.

The Egyptian leader is far past learning from experience; the previous plagues didn't teach him anything. He is long past listening to the advice of his *"officials"* (v. 7). He is willing to risk the destruction of everything and everyone around him because of his vanity. The Bible calls such leaders *"fools"* (v. 2).

Plagues of locusts and darkness are the penultimate signs because they signal de-evolution of creation. As with previous plagues and foolish leadership responses, this is never simply a private matter between the leader and God. Poor leadership responses have consequences that are societal, environmental, and even cosmic.

When a leader lives in darkness long enough, soon there is *"a dense darkness in all the land."* Leadership is a stewardship of creation and chaos, of light and darkness, not only within us, but also around us.

Exercise: *Think of a recent decision you had to make. Evaluate whether the net result of that decision was greater darkness and chaos, or greater light and order. Ask God for the wisdom and tender-heartedness for your next decision to result in more creativity and illumination for those around you.*

John P. Chandler   137

MID-CRIYSIS

WORSHIP PAUSE

"And when your children ask you, "What do you mean by this observance?" you shall say, "It is the Passover sacrifice to the Lord, for he passed over the houses of the Israelites in Egypt, when he struck down the Egyptians but spared our houses." And the people bowed down and worshiped."
– Exodus 12:26-27

The dramatic final encounter of Moses with Pharaoh brackets detailed ritual instructions concerning how Israel is to prepare and celebrate the Passover. The structure looks like this:

- 11:1-10 – Moses' final warnings and predictions;

- 12:1-28 – Elaborate ritual details of the Passover observance which will memorialize what is happening for generations to come;

- 12:29-51 – Predictions about the tenth and final plague come to pass, first-borns die, Israel is spared and departs Egypt with plunder.

The middle section is surprisingly meticulous and detailed for such an urgent situation. Why would Exodus hit the slow-motion button amidst a looming crisis and highlight such seemingly small, precise details as how the lamb should be roasted, the bread unleavened, how observers should be dressed, what they should say, and how blood is to be placed on doorposts (vv. 7ff)?

It is a pattern that will continue throughout Exodus, and is a lesson for Moses and Israel. Every encounter of significance is to be embedded with worship. The ritual markers signify that any decisive action (especially in crisis) is to have at its center the acknowledgement of God as Lord. Before Moses leads the people, before Israel leaves Egypt, everyone stops to worship and acknowledge God as the prime mover and most glorious inhabitant of the community.

Leaders and communities facing urgent situations would do well to embed worship in the midst of confrontation and crisis. Not just before and after encounter – but in the middle.

Exercise: *It is natural for us to pray and worship before and after an urgent confrontation or situation. But now, as you forecast how you will lead in the next crisis, envision how you will pause in the middle of the urgency to worship. Imagine slowing down an urgent situation, marking it ritually, and acknowledging God's Lordship, before re-engaging. Practice this storyline of mid-crisis worship pause until it becomes part of your leadership repertoire.*

Exodus 12-13

"It shall serve as a sign on your hand and as a reminder on your forehead, so that the teaching of the Lord may be on your lips; for with a strong hand the Lord brought you out of Egypt." – Exodus 13:9

The departure story of Israel from Egypt lingers on a detailed description of what an Exodus community will look like. These marks are *"signs"* or *"emblems"* (13:16) of God's newly constituted people:

1. **Journeying** (12:37) – this people will be marked by where it is going more than where it is from.

Praying New Beginnings

2. **Intergenerational** – *"men ... children"* (12:37) – more than the strong are included.

3. ***"Mixed"*** – pedigree now matters less than present and future faithfulness (12:38).

4. **Dependent** – *"nor had they prepared any provisions for themselves"* (12:39); they rely on God to provide for them.

5. **Vigilant** – *"that same night is a vigil to be kept for the Lord by all Israelites throughout their generations"* (12:42). They are watchful, remembering people.

6. **Inclusive but distinctively marked** (12:48) – the resident *"alien"* may be a part of the community, but is *"circumcised"* as a mark of devotion, commitment, and belonging.

7. **"Consecrated" to God** (13:2) – giving *"the firstborn"* reminds the community that all of their life is from God and for God.

8. **Observant** (13:3ff) – Passover is a regular, living reminder of identity.

9. **Storytellers** – *"you shall tell your child on that day"* (13:8) – they are defined by and responsible for transmitting their narrative.

10. **Sacrificial** (13:15) – they are marked by their generosity.

God's Exodus people then and now bear these *"emblems."*

Exercise: *Take inventory of these ten emblems in your life and in the community that you lead. Which two marks are the strongest, and which two are weakest? What might God be saying about you and those you lead in this inventory? How will that affect how you lead today?*

Exodus 14

STAND FIRM | GO FORWARD   BE STILL | CRY OUT

"But Moses said to the people, "Do not be afraid, stand firm, and see the deliverance that the Lord will accomplish for you today; for the Egyptians whom you see today you shall never see again. The Lord will fight for you, and you have only to keep still." Then the Lord said to Moses, "Why do you cry out to me? Tell the Israelites to go forward."
– Exodus 14:13-15

If the resurrection of Jesus is the greatest story of the Bible, then the Exodus of Israel from Egypt is its foreshadowing and closest cousin. It is, as Martin Luther put it, "faith functioning under pressure." Almost exclusively, it narrates a supernatural intervention of God to deliver his people. The story is bracketed by the divine *"pillar of cloud by day/fire by night"* (13:21f and 14:19f), God stepping in miraculously. We learn that God can clog chariot wheels in order to open the hearts of people (v.25)!

It is almost exclusively a story about God's initiative and action. (And so is, incidentally, baptism, which this story foreshadows.) Almost – but not completely. There is a human reaction called for in response to the leadership of God. At the center of it is what God always tells leaders to say to people: *"Do not be afraid."*

To offer this fearless, faithful response, Moses exercises the art of knowing when to tell the people to *"stand firm"* and when to instruct them to *"move forward."* (Another expression of this spectrum is when to *"keep still"* or silent, and when to *"cry out"*). It is the fundamental act of leadership: to dispel fear and activate faith through knowing when to stop or pause, and when to step out into the unknown, when to listen and when to speak.

Moses did this well, and *"the Lord saved Israel that day"* (v. 30). The people *"feared and believed"* (v. 31). Jesus did this in the stillness of the cross and his bursting forth from the tomb. And every act of holy leadership since then has mimicked these models of Moses and Jesus, knowing when to *stand* and when to *move*, when to be *still* and when to *cry out*.

Exercise: *On the spectrum of "stand firm ⟷ go forward" or "be still ⟷ cry out," where are you being called to lead? Mark where you are today … then mark where you are called to lead next. Then pray for the courage to lead in responsiveness to the God who is leading.*

Exodus 15

DEALING WITH WATER

"Then the prophet Miriam, Aaron's sister, took a tambourine in her hand; and all the women went out after her with tambourines and dancing. And Miriam sang to them: "Sing to the Lord, for he has triumphed gloriously; horse and rider he has thrown into the sea." – Exodus 15:20-21

The first stories of Exodus from Egypt and toward the Promised Land are stories about God's salvation through the water. Israel's is a desert faith, and almost any time water is mentioned, it is a symbol for primeval chaos. (Think Noah, Jonah, and Jesus stilling the storm.) Deliverance through the Red Sea is God's grandest act yet of saving his people from the waters of chaos and onto the dry land. No wonder prophet Miriam and leader Moses lead the people to sing of the Lord's glorious triumph! It is a spectacular deliverance and calls for a historic celebration.

Yet on the far side of the sea, there are more water troubles at "*Marah*" (vv. 22ff). After a three day drought, the only drinking water available was "*bitter*" and undrinkable. And where Moses once led his people out of and away from the undrinkable waters of the Nile in Egypt, here, the call was not to leave the water but to stay there, address the situation, and redeem it. So, after prayer, Moses put "*wood*" into the water and it "*became sweet*" and drinkable (v. 25).

Finally, the people camp by "*twelve springs of water*" (v. 27). But they are not to linger by the oasis for long. They are called to journey beyond oasis and through the dry wilderness.

Sometimes leaders are called to take people away from the water (the Nile). Sometimes we lead them through it (the Red Sea). Sometimes we redeem bad water ("*Marah*") and make it "*sweet.*" And sometimes we linger beside it ("*Elim*") and enjoy its refreshment. Exodus people are to deal constantly and artfully with the waters of chaos.

Exercise: *What chaos is confronting you today? How are you called to encounter it, and to lead others to encounter it? To leave it? Go through it? Redeem it? Or dwell within it and be changed by it? Ask God for the discernment to lead through "water" today – whether the Nile, Red Sea, Marah, or Elim.*

John P. Chandler   145

"*The whole congregation of the Israelites complained against Moses and Aaron in the wilderness. The Israelites said to them, "If only we had died by the hand of the Lord in the land of Egypt, when we sat by the fleshpots and ate our fill of bread; for you have brought us out into this wilderness to kill this whole assembly with hunger.*" – Exodus 16:2-3

A food crisis is a faith crisis, and the hunger that threatened Israel's wilderness journey was like the famine that brought them into slavery in Egypt in the first place. It is an urgent situation that needs to be met with an equally urgent leadership response. Their need is legitimate – food. But it is hard to feel much sympathy for the people, when they openly admit that they prefer Egyptian prison food to the radical responsibility finding their own food in a life of freedom. They come off as hard-headed and whiny.

However, as the leader, Moses has to sort out the complaining from the legitimate need. And chapter 16 is a detailed description of the plan for finding daily bread or "*manna.*" Embedded in the plan are great evidences of God's grace and gifts – daily food, freely provided, and even the gift of a weekly Sabbath rest (vv. 22ff), complete with extra food. Of course, the people are non-compliant (v. 27), stubborn, and ungrateful. But they are able to march on, because they are given a clear outline of how their basic needs for food, rest, and a schedule will be met.

Even whiners have real needs. Every person legitimately can hope to know where their next meal might come from, whether the future will be more promising than the past, and whether there will be rest from their hard routine. Moses leads well because he sorts out these real needs from the murmuring which can drive a leader crazy. Leadership always involves the art of drowning out the background noise of complaint to listen and respond to the real needs underneath the whining of those we lead.

Exercise: *Can you distinguish between the whining of those you lead from their real needs? Make a short list of which complaints against you represent simple immaturity, and which point to legitimate hopes. Ask God for the grace to ignore the former and respond to the latter today.*

Exodus 17

HELP FOR

CHRONIC FATIGUE

"Whenever Moses held up his hand, Israel prevailed;
whenever he lowered his hand, Amalek prevailed. But Moses'
hands grew weary; so they took a stone and put it under him,
and he sat on it. Aaron and Hur held up his hands, one on
one side and the other on the other side; so his hands were
steady until the sun set. And Joshua defeated Amalek with
the sword." – Exodus 17:11-13

Leadership is not simply moving happy people from one oasis to the next. Water questions are about concrete support for life and whether God is present, and Moses is charged with moving ungrateful and forgetful people through drought. Their complaining is so incessant that he named the towns "*Massah and Meribah*" (v. 7, meaning "test" and "find fault") to memorialize their bickering!

Simultaneously, Israel now faces external attack from a fierce desert enemy, the Amalekites. Everything rises and falls with

Praying New Beginnings

leadership, and this is symbolized in Moses' hands. When his arms were lifted, the battle turned to Israel; when they fell, Amalek surged. What a burden to be so responsible, and how draining the constant responsibility of point leadership!

It is understandably fatiguing, and the most noteworthy feature of the story is how Moses' took measures to deal with both his extraordinary responsibility and very-ordinary humanity. Because Moses' leadership was irreplaceable and task-critical, it was he who had to hold up his hands. The actual task of fighting could be delegated to Joshua, but spiritual point-leadership could not be farmed out to anyone else. The unrelenting responsibility to lift his hands was very tiring. And the fatigue of the leader would impact decisively the outcome of the battle and the fate of the people.

The story does not tell whose idea it was to seat Moses and place two people around him. But the decision to support the leader who was subject to potentially lethal fatigue was a battle-changer. Those who want to lead well, lead through battles, and lead beyond the ups-and-downs of our humanity are wisest when they have people around them to mitigate the effects of chronic fatigue on the leader and on the people s/he leads.

Exercise: *When are you most impacted by "H.A.L.T." (hungry, angry, lonely, tired)? When are you most at risk within a day, over the course of a week, and in certain times of the year? Write down those times when you are typically at risk. Then, for each time (daily, weekly, seasonal) write the names of two people who can be supportive and refreshing to you in each of those three at-risk zones. Make a plan to ask those people for their help as you anticipate them – and lean on them when you need them!*

TOO HEAVY A TASK FOR ONE PERSON

"Why do you sit alone, while all the people stand around you from morning until evening? ... What you are doing is not good. You will surely wear yourself out, both you and these people with you. For the task is too heavy for you; you cannot do it alone." – Exodus 18:14, 17-18

Leading a revolution is one thing, but governing ornery victors is another. Moses is trying to govern like a tribal chief, and his mode of decision-making is threatening to destroy both him and the mission. Sometimes the leader is right, the mission is right, but the mode is wrong.

In steps his father-in-law, Jethro. With a combination of wisdom and revelation, he gently confronts Moses' style of leadership – and, better yet, points him toward a better way. It is one of the richest treasure troves of leadership counsel in the Bible. Lessons include:

1. Three high costs for a leadership style overly dependent on a charismatic leader are:
   a. Bureaucracy (*"people stood around him from morning until evening"*)
   b. Exhaustion of the leader (*"you will wear yourself out"*)
   c. Untapped and unproductive potential leaders (*"people stand around you"*).
2. Leaders need trusted and wise counselors, as Jethro was to Moses.
3. Spiritual leadership can borrow insights from other modes of leading (in this case, Jethro's military model of organization).
4. Charismatic leaders can be trapped by over-reliance on their own gifts and stay with outmoded forms of leading too long.
5. The greatest untapped leadership resources are typically the under-utilized potential leaders who *"stand around you"* – and if you over-function, they will under-function.
6. Leaders have to accept that most of their work is not dramatic (invoking plagues or going through the Red Sea) but learning to excel in day-to-day judgment calls (vv. 22ff).
7. Once you empower other leaders around you, the mission can continue (vv. 24-27).

Leading well is usually *"too heavy a task for one person."* It takes the full-functioning gifts of many leaders to govern and guide a people and a mission through the wilderness.

Exercise: *Beside each of the seven lessons above, place a checkmark if a strength and an "x" if a weakness you have as a daily decision-maker. How do you need to grow in the next season of your life in response to this scorecard? For today, in at least a small way, aim to highlight one of your checked strengths, and make a small gain in one of the marked weaknesses.*

"Then Moses went up to God; the Lord called to him from the mountain, saying, "Thus you shall say to the house of Jacob, and tell the Israelites: You have seen what I did to the Egyptians, and how I bore you on eagles' wings and brought you to myself." – Exodus 19:3-4

After the Red Sea, Moses leads the people at a pretty good clip through the desert and toward the Promised Land. But here at the foot of Mount Sinai, there is a significant pause. Israel will spend the rest of the book of Exodus (and Leviticus and Numbers) working out the "*covenant*" (v. 5) God makes with them. Forty years of wandering in the wilderness, working out what it means that while *"the whole earth"* belongs to God, his covenant people were to be a *"treasured possession out of all the peoples,"* or a *"priestly kingdom and holy nation"* (vv. 5f).

God describes to Moses the divine way of leading as bearing people up *"on eagles' wings."* Walter Brueggemann disabuses us of any romantic notions about the nobility of eagles by reminding us that the Hebrew word can also suggest "vulture." Either way, God swoops down with bird-of-prey talons and craving onto a left-for-dead people and takes them into the air!

A mother eagle will drop her young mid-flight to "test" them and see if they can fly. She will swoop in to rescue them if not, and surely God has done this for his people out of Egypt. But the mother *wants* the young to fly on their own, so she does not over-rescue and enable constant dependence. She is willing to put the young at risk and in discomfort.

Moses is to lead in this eagle-like manner as well, imitating the way God leads. And we can learn from the metaphor that leading is not romantic soaring but constant testing and pushing. It is not about how many babies we can carry on our backs, but how many of our released young have learned to fly on their own.

Exercise: *If we measure our leadership by who is "flying on their own," how are we doing? Whom are we testing and releasing, rescuing only as preparation? Are we over-rescuing and intervening to enable ongoing dependence? Or are we helping those we lead to grow up? As you think of someone in whom you are investing your life, give yourself a score from one to ten that ranks how you are doing with them on this matter. And then ask God to show you what you need to do today to raise your score by one point.*

SUNGLASSES

FOR AN UNDISTORTED LIFE

"I am the Lord your God who brought you out of the land of Egypt, out of the house of slavery; you shall have no other gods before me." – Exodus 20:2-3

This is the great covenant between God and his people, the Lord and his subjects, a statement of the divine grace that calls forth a grateful obedience in response. The Red Sea leads to this "bill of rights" as boundary markers for a free life in a Promised Land. Law is grounded in story and grace. Deliverance *"out of the land of Egypt"* is the context for a life-code that will lead to an expansive, not restrictive, life together.

In his sermon, "*Called Against the Distortion*," Walter Brueggemann says that the commandments are "God's abiding markers against all distortions of life that are sure to occur when the holy reality of God is displaced from the center of our existence." Given our "deeply distorted society" (then and now), such work is an "incredibly upstream vocation." This helps us to imagine the Ten Commandments as a lens, a set of sunglasses, that clarifies reality, filters glare, and helps us to see God, our world, and ourselves rightly within it:

It is the call of God's people to live clearly. Not just religious professionals but ordinary decision-makers wear these glasses. Leaders function to remind people to put on their sunglasses. When we do so, we see not simply what seems to be (because of societal distortion), but what <u>really</u> is (God's reality), in its truest light.

Exercise: *Given the choices you need to make today, which of the four dimensions mentioned above need to be your lead lens for decision-making? Do you need to make decisions worshipfully or with <u>reverence</u>? Choose in light of <u>remembering</u> what God has graciously done for you? Consider the wider community <u>respectfully</u>? Or think in terms of guarding holy <u>reputation</u>? All will be factors, but pray through your decisions now in the light of one of these four.*

Exodus 21

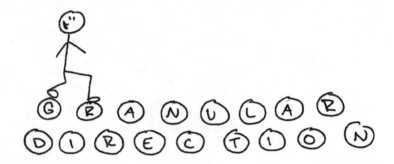

"If any harm follows, then you shall give them life for life, eye for eye, tooth for tooth, hand for hand, foot for foot, burn for burn, wound for wound, stripe for stripe."
– Exodus 21:23-24

From the sweeping grandeur of the Ten Commandments, the next chapters of Exodus jump into the gritty matters of everyday life. It is as jarring as reading the "Bill of Rights" one minute to reading the fine print of a legal document in the next.

Much has been made of the specifics of the "Covenant Code." On the one hand, the fact that parts of it were used in the United States to defend slavery (v. 21) have led some to dismiss the validity of all of it as ancient, brutish, tribal law. On the other hands, some scholars recognize the *lex talionis* of "*eye for eye, tooth for tooth*" as a major ethical leap forward, an early advance in the Bible's scheme of progressive revelation and redemption. "*Eye for eye*" served to limit retribution and broke cycles of revenge through equality. It has been a foundation for administering justice for millennia since.

I have a friend who, when I try to make sweeping statements about what I hope to accomplish, chides me to become more "granular." That is, he wants not just lofty vision but specific details of how I plan to carry things out. He asks how I am going to work out vision in day-to-day life.

From a leadership lens, Exodus 21 is valuable because it is "granular." An observant leader can descend from mountain-top vision-casting to spelling out day-to-day codes of how we are going to live and move together. Granular direction is how vision works its way into reality.

Exercise: *Write down one great hope you have for a leadership or relationship situation. Now under what you have written down, list three specific steps you will take toward it: one for today, one for this week, and one for this month. Focus on executing these small steps. Once you have done this, review, and repeat with other big goals as necessary.*

Exodus 22

ALIENS.   WIDOWS,   ORPHANS

"You shall not wrong or oppress a resident alien, for you were aliens in the land of Egypt. You shall not abuse any widow or orphan." – Exodus 22:21-22

Life together requires house rules, and rules require interpretation. Exodus 22 is a series of interpretations about "case law" – what to do in ambiguous or socially unacceptable cases or situations that inevitably arise when people are in close proximity.

Much of the case law was period-specific – for instance, *"you shall not permit a female sorcerer to live"* (v. 18) – and not translatable to contemporary leadership situations. Yet it is unwise to throw the baby out with the bathwater, and to dismiss <u>all</u> of case law as irrelevant because <u>some</u> of it applied only to ancient Israel is foolishness. The way forward is to follow the Bible itself in its example: it tries to boil down core principles and apply them across the board to grey situations.

Those core principles in chapter 22 can be simply stated:

1. <u>Administer justice</u> – deal with carelessness (21:33ff), theft (22:1-4), neglect (vv. 5f), trusteeship (vv. 7-15); and

2. <u>Protect the vulnerable</u> – the *"resident alien,"* *"widow,"* and *"orphan"* merit special attention and protection.

Following the example of biblical case law, a leader today must speak for justice and especially so for those who have no voice to defend themselves. This is just as true today as in ancient Israel, and a leader who neglects to guard the defenseless will have to deal with a God who insists we do so.

Exercise: *Who is the most at-risk and vulnerable person in your circle of influence? As you envision the face of this individual in prayer, ask God to guide you in ensuring justice for this person. Make sure the sun does not set today before you have spoken out in a way that makes a difference on their behalf.*

Exodus 23

SEASONS OF FESTIVAL

"Three times in the year you shall hold a festival for me."
– Exodus 23:14

The heart of Exodus 23 consists of detailed instructions about Israel's use of <u>time</u>. First, there are reminders about the weekly *"sabbath"* (v. 12). Sabbath is the key way that Israel will remember to *"be attentive"* to God, to resist idolatry, and to be careful with their language (*"not invoke the names of other gods,"* v. 13).

Praying New Beginnings

Then, there is the command to mark three annual *"festivals"* – a remembrance of the Passover, and two harvest festivals (Pentecost and the feast of Booths). It seems an unusual requirement for a sojourning people, marching through the wilderness and looking for their home in the Promised Land. But coming on the heels of the Ten Commandments, rebooting the annual calendar by marking it with Sabbath and these three festivals must be important. Why so?

The wisdom here is that identity is connected to rhythm of life, and rhythm is determined by how we spend our days, weeks, and seasons. One way to remember who God is and what God has done for us, and to remember our identity in a strange land, is to mark our lives by scheduled celebrations. Both Sabbath and festival are very "unproductive." However, the people of God are not defined by what they produce. We are who we are by the gifts we have received from a gracious God. Sabbath and festival enact and celebrate that identity.

Despite outcries of "inefficiency!" and "cost!" a good leader will schedule festival markers. These help us remember that we are, at the core, chosen and blessed people.

Exercise: *What are the ritual festivals scheduled in your life this year? (Or are there any?) What do they celebrate? How does your annual calendar describe your identity? Deliberate on your annual schedule, and if there need to be corrections made so that you have space for festivals, make those changes.*

MARKERS OF PROMISE

"Moses took the blood and dashed it on the people, and said, "See the blood of the covenant that the Lord has made with you in accordance with all these words." – Exodus 24:8

Exodus 24 is about the ceremonial ratification of a covenant between God and Israel. Moses and the elders are summoned, with great seriousness, to *"read"* and *"hear"* the Law from God that will order their distinctive lives. To highlight the occasion, there are significant ritual actions:

- Solemn reading of vows – not unlike our wedding ceremonies today;

- Blood exchange – there is a sacrifice, altar, and blood sprinkled on the people;

- Ceremonial meal – the leaders *"ate and drank"* (v. 11).

After these solemn ceremonies, the people *"saw the God of Israel"* (vv. 10, 17).

We have precious few ceremonial markers –the exchange of vows and rings at a wedding, or national flag rituals are rare remnants. North Americans are typically far too pragmatic for fussy ceremonies. And we don't have to have a ceremony for every time we promise to pick up milk at the store. But there is a time and place to make life-altering promises, and a good leader leads people to mark those covenants with enacted rituals.

Exercise: *Have you thought seriously about how to mark key promises or covenants with those around you ceremonially? Is there a vow, exchange, meal, or other symbol that you might use to do so? Ask God to show you a concrete way today to symbolize a covenant-promise in your life and leadership.*

"*The Lord said to Moses: Tell the Israelites to take for me an offering; from all whose hearts prompt them to give you shall receive the offering for me.*" – **Exodus 25:1-2**

It took Genesis only two chapters to describe the creation of the world. But when it comes time for Exodus to describe the creation of the tabernacle and its implements, six chapters are necessary. Overall, nearly one-third of Exodus is devoted to describing the tabernacle (chapters 25-31, 39-40). Apparently building the people of God around proper acknowledgement of God is more important and more complex than creation of the earth!

Among other things, the intense focus on the tabernacle signals a change in the way God is going to be present with his people. This makes the opening statement about the tabernacle significant; it is to be built by means of "*an offering from all whose hearts prompt me them to give.*" At its foundation, the tabernacle will be a structure organically proceeding from responsive, generous hearts. Biblically, God's nearness is always connected to heart-receptivity and responding generosity.

As Moses was to hear God's call to stir the generous and open people to give liberally, so leaders ever since have been and will be called to do so. Leaders unashamedly ask those who have the heart for it to respond with offerings. It is not forcing the unwilling or manipulating the stingy. But leaders prompt those with tender hearts to turn loose of all kinds of "*gems*" (vv. 3-7) for God's "*sanctuary*" in order that "*God may dwell among them*" (v. 8).

Exercise: *What acts of generosity do you need to prompt in those around you today? Who has a receptive heart to give? Your prayerful contribution may be to call them to give it.*

John P. Chandler 165

Exodus 26-27

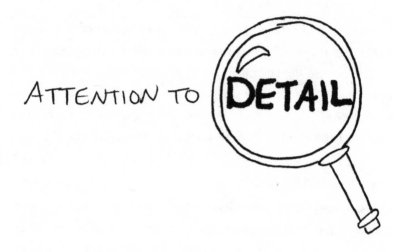

*"Then you shall erect the tabernacle according to the plan
for it that you were shown on the mountain."*
– Exodus 26:30

God gives two major sets of instructions to his Exodus people:
one concerning the Law (the ethical), the other about the Tabernacle
(the liturgical). The seven speeches of Exodus 25-31 mirror the
seven days of creation, with both ending in Sabbath.

The attention to construction detail here is critical. This is the hallowing of space and time. God is now going to be present in the midst of the people and not on the top of the mountain. God is not to be found in a fixed shrine but is portable and on a journey with the people.

And perhaps most importantly, the elaborate construction instructions – given from God on the mountain – signal that worship is not a matter about which details can be neglected. If the people of God are careless in constructing worship, where else might they be inattentive? It is a slippery slope to accommodation, syncretism, apostasy, and idolatry.

Many "visionary leaders" today proudly trumpet their lack of care about the details of their vision. It is certainly possible to miss the forest for the trees. But some things are so central and vital that to skim carelessly over the fine details is to miss the point. Like Moses, a good leader today knows when to slow down the march, go over the fine print, and impress upon the people the centrality of the most vital things that shape who they are and where they are going.

Exercise: *When have you been careless with the details about something important, and what did it cost you and/or others? Reflect on that experience, and ask God to impress upon you when and how to slow down and take your time with details in a leadership situation today. Write down those details ahead of time, execute them, and then review at the end of the day.*

John P. Chandler

THE LEADER'S CLOTHES

"So Aaron shall bear the names of the sons of Israel in the breastplate of judgment on his heart when he goes into the holy place, for a continual remembrance before the Lord."
– Exodus 28:29

"Clothes make the man," said many who wanted me, as a teenager, to dress up. "Clothes make the man *warmer,*" said my best friend Glynn, mocking the sentiment about dressing to impress. How is the leader to think about the clothes s/he wears?

Exodus 28 is an unexpected source of help as it describes the vestments Aaron and other priests are to wear. The details of colors, ornamentation, and fabric are situation-specific. But we see a principle greater than the specifics in verse 29. Amidst details about *"ephods"* and *"breastpieces,"* Exodus tells us the clothing *"bears the names of the sons of Israel"* and *"the judgment of the Israelites on his heart before the Lord continually"* (v. 30). Above all else, in other words, the leader's clothing reflects thoughtfulness about the people as they stand before God. The clothes of the leader are mindful of the people led and of the God before whom they are led.

First Peter 3:4 later corrects overly-flashy dressers with the words, *"rather, let your adornment be the inner self with the lasting beauty of a gentle and quiet spirit, which is very precious in God's sight."* The leader doesn't just wear whatever s/he wants. Instead, our clothing reflects mindfulness about the people we are leading and the God continually before us. The outer clothes reflect the *"inner self."* We don't simply pick clothes according to personal tastes; our role before other people and especially the *"judgment"* of God govern us.

We do, indeed, "dress to impress." But we dress to impress God first, with those we lead therefore continually on our hearts.

Exercise: *How are you going to pick out what you wear this week? Beyond obvious factors (weather, what is clean), how can you be intentional about letting your clothing choices be leadership-appropriate, with the people you lead and the God you serve foremost in mind?*

Exodus 29

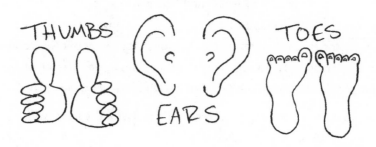

THE LEADER'S THUMBS EARS TOES

"And you shall slaughter the ram, and take some of its blood and put it on the lobe of Aaron's right ear and on the lobes of the right ears of his sons, and on the thumbs of their right hands, and on the big toes of their right feet, and dash the rest of the blood against all sides of the altar."
– Exodus 29:20

Amidst obscure details of ancient rituals of animal sacrifice lies a great and still-worthy principle: God commits to his journeying people an ongoing intimacy and closeness. These ceremonial *"offerings"* enact *"atonement"* (v. 36) or *"at-one-ment."* They put the people "at one" with the God whom they serve and who is leading them through the wilderness toward the Promised Land.

The *"priests"* (*"Aaron and his sons"*) are *"consecrated"* to lead people to remember the continual watchfulness of God over their lives. To that end, the ordination service for these leaders takes the life-symbolizing blood of the ram and puts some upon the priests' *"lobes of the right ears," "thumbs of their right hands,"* and *"big toes of their right feet."* Each body part is a metaphor for the core work of these leaders:

- *Ears* – the work of leaders is first to listen … to God and to the people;

- *Thumbs* – what the leader puts his or her "right hand" or core tasks to do is consecrated first to God;

- *Toes* – the leader will be mindful about where s/he goes, careful that wherever s/he steps will be a journey of mediating God's intimate presence among the people.

In my Baptist tradition, we celebrate the "priesthood of all believers" – the idea that because Jesus Christ is our only mediator between God and humanity, all of us have been commissioned to function as priests. We all lead in some sense. And thus, in our daily priestly decisions, we consecrate our *"ears, thumbs, and toes"* to the work of communicating the close presence of God for those whom we lead.

Exercise: *Of the three core centers of "priestly" leadership, where do you most need to be attentive as a decision-maker today? Do you need to focus on your listening <u>ear</u>? Putting your right hand (<u>thumb</u>) to some key task? Or do your key leadership requirements today pertain to where your feet (toes) take you? Meditate on your "ear, thumb, and toe." Ask God to direct you regarding your priestly work today. Pray over your right ear, right thumb, and/or right toe – and consecrate yourself to using them well today in whatever you lead.*

Exodus 30

MERCY SEAT

"You shall place it in front of the curtain that is above the ark of the covenant, in front of the mercy seat, where I will meet with you." – Exodus 30:6

Most of the now-obscure ritual details of Exodus 30 – concerning *"altar, incense, census money, spices"* – pertain to the annual *"rite of atonement."* The spiritual leader's job is to reconcile the sinful people with their holy Lord. Without such relational healing, the people cannot continue their journey through wilderness to the Promised Land.

Central to atonement (at-one-ment) is construction of a *"mercy seat."* It is placed alongside the *"ark of the covenant"* which contains the promises of God and proper responses of the people. When promise/response is in order, there is *"covenant."* The *"mercy seat"* is thus the focal point at which God *"will meet with you."* It's an amazing thought – that the God of the universe is uniquely present at a physical place where covenant and reconciliation are renewed.

While such a ritual space is unique to Israel's desert experience, there is wisdom for leaders today to consecrate a *"mercy seat."* Mediators teach us that when people are estranged, the odds of reconciliation are best when the conversations are framed within a set-apart space. When a leader can create a safe place for unstable or volatile relational reconciliation, s/he mediates well.

We can identify and guide people to a mercy seat. There they can meet with the God of the covenant. When those meetings reaffirm our core promises from God and to God, they lead to healing and wholeness of all kinds.

Exercise: *Envision a "mercy seat," a site where you can physically go (and take others) to set things right. (I have a "chair of care" in which I seat people to pray for them.) Consecrate that space/seat for the work of God in human life. Communicate to others what it is for. And be mindful to use that space the next time there is need for a leadership conversation to set things right.*

 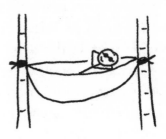

SKILLFUL
CRAFT

TIMELY
REST

*"I have filled him with divine spirit, with ability, intelligence,
and knowledge in every kind of craft, to devise artistic
designs ... I have given skill to all the skillful, so that they
may make all that I have commanded you."*
– Exodus 31:3f, 6

Clearly, as the writer of Exodus describes the construction of the worship life of journeying Israel, he wants us to think of the creation of the world in Genesis 1. The chapter ends with the seventh of seven speeches (Exodus 25-31), and just as on the seventh day of creation God rested, verses 12-17 demand timely rest or *"Sabbath."* It is in the created order of things. It is not optional. It is commanded on *"tablets of stone, written with the finger of God"* (v. 18).

But leading up to that rest, there is work to be done. And the work of crafting the tabernacle and its implements is not to be a haphazard afterthought, but to be done by those whom God has *"given skill"* (v. 6). So Moses is to call out very specific people (*"Bezalel,"* v. 1 and *"Oholiab,"* v. 6) to do the craft-work, because God has *"filled him with divine spirit,"* the same Spirit that hovered over the waters of creation in Genesis 1:2. The crafter's work will reflect *"ability, intelligence, knowledge"* and artistry. Later, Exodus 35:34 will describe their work as *"inspired"* and something that *"teaches"* others.

We are clearly not to work all of the time; the Sabbath is God's gift to us. But when we do God's work, we are to deploy the greatest level of artistry or craft. Clearly there are all sorts of God-given abilities and intelligences. The good leader finds those with God-given artistic ability and sets them up to showcase their craftwork for the glory of God.

Exercise: *Identify at least two people around you who have unusual ability as artists or crafters. How can you call on them to bring their skill to bear on a project that will result in a beautiful creation that glorifies God?*

CAPITULATION
OR
INTER VENTION

*"When Moses saw that the people were running wild
(for Aaron had let them run wild, to the derision of their
enemies), then Moses stood in the gate of the camp and said,
"Who is on the Lord's side? Come to me!"*
– Exodus 32:25-26

After seven speeches of exacting requirements for walking in covenant with God, Israel has heard enough. They punt. They want nothing of meticulous work and demanding relationship. So they find a more accommodating "leader" in Aaron. It is easier just to have Aaron melt down their golden jewelry, fashion an idol that requires nothing of them, and go with that. *"These are your gods,"* they say (vv. 4, 8). They have a party and *"revel"* (v. 6). Aaron simply lets the people *"run wild"* and takes no responsibility. He excuses his complicity in the situation by telling Moses that he simply gathered the gold, *"threw it into the fire, and out came this calf!"* (vv. 24f) How about that?! Aaron completely panders and capitulates to what the people want.

We see a very different picture of leadership in Moses. He does not simply cave in to what the people want. He negotiates with God to *"change your mind"* and *"not bring disaster on your people"* (v. 12). Though personally, his *"anger burned hot"* (v. 19), Moses has the hard conversations with God, and makes the hard decisions with the people to set the situation right. He orders the faithful to purge the corrupted tribe of their fatal disease (vv. 26-29). It is the first of many times Moses does the hard work of repair and mediation through interceding for *"atonement for your sin"* (v. 30).

A person of position can give people exactly what they want, as Aaron did. Or that leader, like Moses, can hold people accountable to the most demanding yet rewarding relationship they can have – their covenant with God. The fate of the people's journey toward the Promised Land depends on the willingness of the leader to have the hard conversations and make the hard decisions, intervening decisively in order to uphold covenant relationship.

Exercise: *In what situation are you tempted to be too passive and compliant? Where might God be calling you to intervene, though it will be difficult and costly? Pray as hard as Moses prayed in Exodus 32. Work on your own anger. And ask God to help you intervene as a leader in this hard place rather than take the easy path of avoidance.*

"*And while my glory passes by I will put you in a cleft of the rock, and I will cover you with my hand until I have passed by; then I will take away my hand, and you shall see my back; but my face shall not be seen.*"
– **Exodus 33:22-23**

Furious with a *"stiff-necked people"* (v. 3), God tells Moses that he is substituting an angel for his own direct accompanying presence. Were he to get too close, God would *"consume"* them. Where the ark of the covenant previous symbolized the closeness of God amidst the people (chapter 25), now Moses goes to the *"tent of meeting"* which is *"outside the camp"* to speak with God. There God will *"speak to Moses face to face, as one speaks to a friend"* (vv. 7-11). Israel? Not so much.

The climactic scene in vv. 12-23 has Moses, in direct conversation with God, requesting God to show his *"glory."* God offers to allow his *"goodness"* and *"name"* to pass before Moses, but not his *"face."* So God hides Moses in a cave-like *"cleft,"* passes by, and allows Moses to see his *"back"* but not his direct *"face."*

It is a study of God's simultaneous closeness and distance from his people, the divine immanence and transcendence. God is not remote but neither is he our homeboy. God wants to direct and guide his people, but God is of a different order of being than the rest of us. This story of God's distance from us is a reminder for leaders who seek guidance never to be casual in approaching a holy and righteous God. In our interactions with God, we can get close – but not too close.

Exercise: *As you look to God for guidance today, think of ways that you can acknowledge his holy difference from us. Worship God, and do not simply treat him as a buddy. Be aware of the transcendent, glorious presence of the Lord of the universe as you pray now, and throughout the day.*

John P. Chandler   179

Exodus 34

GLOW-RY!

"Whenever Moses went in before the Lord to speak with him, he would take the veil off, until he came out; and when he came out, and told the Israelites what he had been commanded, the Israelites would see the face of Moses, that the skin of his face was shining ...."
– Exodus 34:34-35

The story line of the Bible is that the God of the heavens breaks into our earthly reality, encounters us, and we are transformed. Walter Brueggemann says, "The Bible is organized around the explosive moments when the holiness of God touches down in our midst and changes everything." This "eruption of the holy," in Moses' case caused his face to glow. *"The skin of his face shone because he had been talking with God"* (v. 29). Needless to say, this caused Israel to hear listen intently to the commandments from God that Moses relayed to them. Wouldn't you?

The old southern preachers of my youth, in exaggerated accent, used to pronounce the "glory" of God as "glow-ry." It's an illuminating pun (sorry!). God's *glory* impacts a human being in such a way that they have a kind of "glow" or "shine." We undergo metamorphosis and are seen differently by people around us because of our transformational and conversational relationship with God. There is a residue of our encounter with God visible to others. So Paul would later write,

> *"And all of us, with unveiled faces, seeing the glory of the Lord as though reflected in a mirror, are being transformed into the same image from one degree of glory to another; for this comes from the Lord, the Spirit."* – 2 Corinthians 3:18

A leader who has encountered God's glory personally will be viewed by others as glowing or shining in some way. This is a person who has been transformed, and out of that experience has something to offer to others to illumine the way.

Prayer: *"God of grace and God of glory, come to me as you did to Moses. Speak with me today. Let your face shine upon me, and let my face shine to others because of it. Let me somehow glow today as a reflection of your nature and character in my encounters with others, so that they may see you as I have seen you, and be changed. In the name of Jesus, the exact imprint of your being, Amen."*

John P. Chandler 181

Exodus 35

GENEROUS HEARTS AND SKILLED HANDS

"All the Israelite men and women whose hearts made them willing to bring anything for the work that the Lord had commanded by Moses to be done, brought it as a freewill offering to the Lord." – Exodus 35:29

Exodus 35-40 is a "re-do." After God gives the Ten Commandments and the Law to Israel – and then Israel discards them in favor of a golden calf – Moses must patiently lead by rebuilding the community shattered in self-destruction. It is unglamorous, detailed work. Chapters 35-40 tediously detail the fine print that works out what was commanded in the seven speeches of chapters 25-31.

The first command to rebuild community is the *"Sabbath of solemn rest"* (v. 2). The time signature of the community's new song will be a worshipful rhythm of life that begins with honoring and acknowledging God.

Then come multiple mentions of the people who *"bring the Lord's offering"* (vv. 4, 21, 29). It is the most highlighted feature of chapter 35. Whether *"men or women"* (v. 29), whether gifts of *"all sorts of gold objects"* (v. 22) or gifts of *"skill"* or *"artisan design"* (vv. 26, 35), the people are to give an offering of their possessions and talents.

And they do! Again and again, the story highlights how people are moved by *"generous hearts"* to use their *"skillful hands."* They gladly return their God-given possessions and talents to rebuild a new and re-centered community. Such a community, like project leader *"Bezalel,"* is *"filled with divine spirit, with skill, intelligence, and knowledge of every kind of craft, to devise artistic designs"* (vv. 30-32).

This is a vision toward which every leader can aspire: to mobilize generous hearts in many willing people, deploying their gifts for the reconstruction of a beautiful community centered in life that acknowledges God in time and space.

Exercise: *As you envision what God is calling you to lead, who are the people around you who are willing to help, and what are some of the gifts they have that will be useful in accomplishing that vision? Make a list of some of the "generous hearts" and "skilled hands" around you. Pray for these people. Ask God to show you how these willing people can contribute to the creation of a beautiful community.*

Exodus 36

MORE THAN ENOUGH TO DO ALL THE WORK

"So the people were restrained from bringing; for what they had already brought was more than enough to do all the work." – Exodus 36:6-7

The work of rebuilding broken Israel was mind-numbingly extensive. Chapters 35-40 describe elaborate and exacting renovations of worship space, ritual calendar, dress code, and record-keeping. The sheer detail of all that had to be redone was overwhelming.

Moses is the initiating point leader for the project. His role is to jump-start it with two key visionary commands (sabbath-keeping and a call for the generous to bring and offering). And then, he disappears until the end of the project (39:43). Off stage goes Moses; on stage come craftsmen *"Bezalel and Oholiab"* (vv. 1ff). More than those two, on stage come all of the people who bring not only their artistic and carpentry abilities, but also the financial backing to carry off the project. They brought so much that Moses' final act of leadership was to *"restrain"* the givers because of the surplus of *"freewill offerings"* (vv. 2-7)! Can you imagine having to tell people to stop being so overwhelmingly generous?

Often leadership involves inspiring people to step up to meet the challenges of time and money necessary to accomplish a visionary task. But Exodus 36 is a reminder that, among the people of God, there are many, many leaders who bring many, many gifts. There is more than enough capacity in any group we lead to do astounding things. The point-leader's job is to call people to lead and give, to step out of the way and let others drive the project, and (if necessary) contain the scope of their generosity. We who lead don't lead out of scarcity. We don't have to do it all on our own. God's people have *"more than enough"* to do the work. Call on them!

Exercise: *Meditate deeply on the phrase, "more than enough" now. As you work through leadership challenges this week, look for opportunities to prompt and deploy the gifts of the people around you. Come back continually to the idea that God will provide "more than enough" through the people to do all the work.*

INTERPRETING THE DETAILS

"When Moses saw that they had done all the work just as the Lord had commanded, he blessed them."
– Exodus 39:43

Biblical interpreters historically have attributed elaborate symbolic significance to the construction details of the tabernacle and its implements. In many churches today, you may still hear teaching about it: the *"incense"* is a symbol for the Holy Spirit; *"crimson yarn"* is the blood of the Messiah, etc. Some allegories are, to put it mildly, a "reach." But occasionally, Exodus itself suggests clues: *"There were twelve stones with names corresponding to the names of the sons of Israel"* (39:14).

Clearly repeated in the text is that all the work was completed "as the Lord had commanded Moses" (39:1, 5, 7, 21, 29, 31, 43; the phrase is repeated eighteen times altogether in chapters 35-40). The details mean *something*. As Richard Foster says,

> "No doubt some of the interpretations have been fanciful. Yet the exercise is not without its spiritual value. You get the sense from Scripture that God does nothing on a whim. Everything has a purpose. There is a significance to what he chooses. We are right to suspect the furniture of his house is more than just functional décor … Everything he has made says something about (God) ….Acacia wood says something about him. And gold. And the metals that form bronze. And yarn spun from the hair of goats. God, because he is invisible, must be a god of symbols and representations and sacraments if he is going to communicate himself to the human race."

No doubt we can go too far in attributing deep meaning to every esoteric detail around us. But part of the leader's work is to make sense of what is around us. We speak of the holy significance captured in ordinary things and events. We do so with restraint and without being bizarre. But when we can name the deeper importance of an ordinary thing around us, we serve to remind those we lead of the thorough-going presence of the divine in our lives and world.

Exercise: *Pause this morning to observe some details around your prayer setting right now. (For me, it is the desk upon which I write, and a tree I planted outside my window.) Muse on the deeper symbolism of these ordinary things. Ask God to reveal something of the same sense of sacrament as you go through the day – and speak of it to one other person before the day is done.*

Exodus 40

*"For the cloud of the Lord was on the tabernacle by day,
and fire was in the cloud by night, before the eyes of all
the house of Israel at each stage of their journey."*
– Exodus 40:38

Nine months after arriving at Sinai, the *"tabernacle"* is born (v. 17). Anticipating the book of Leviticus, priests, not Moses, now stand in the gap between God and Israel. The priests mediate God's holy presence in a place which serves as a vehicle for God to be close to the people, but not the same as the people. Later, the

New Testament would describe Jesus in the same immanent yet transcendent way: *"For in him all the fullness of God was pleased to dwell, and through him God was pleased to reconcile to himself all things, whether on earth or in heaven, by making peace through the blood of his cross"* (Colossians 1:19-20).

But while the tabernacle is the place for the *"cloud"* and *"fire"* of God's presence, this tabernacle is not a fixed shrine. There is no always-and-forever pilgrimage to Sinai. Rather, God's presence is on the move: *"Whenever the cloud was taken up from the tabernacle, the Israelites would set out on each stage of the journey"* (v. 36). Neither God nor God's people are to be static, but have *"stage(s) of their journey."* Significantly, the last word of the book of Exodus is *"journey."* The story has movement, pilgrimage, *exodus* as its climactic theme.

So *"Moses finished the work"* (v. 33), yet God and his people are still on a *"journey."* There are finish lines, yet work to be done; milestones, but a trip to be taken; accomplishments completed but ongoing work to do. Then and now, the work of the leader is to finish some things, and then look ahead to the rest of the journey. The art of leading is to be truly done with some chapters … and then move on toward the rest of the book.

Exercise: *Name a recent "finish line" that marks the completion of something important in your life and the lives of those whom you influence. What and when is the next "finish line?" Mark down the dates of those two milestones on a calendar. Give thanks to God for the completion of one. Ask God for the grace to move toward the next. Then note whether it is more difficult for you to <u>complete</u> a chapter of life and leadership, or to envision and <u>move on</u> to the next chapter of the journey.*

Leviticus 1

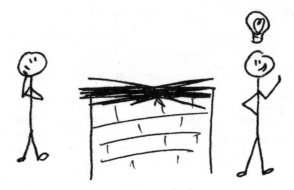

INVENTIVE WAYS TO SACRIFICE

"The Lord summoned Moses and spoke to him from the tent of meeting, saying: Speak to the people of Israel and say to them: When any of you bring an offering of livestock to the Lord, you shall bring your offering from the herd or from the flock." – Leviticus 1:1-2

The painstakingly detailed work of tabernacle construction concludes the book of Exodus. Leviticus then describes what will go on in this place where God and people meet. What will be the prime business transacted there?

Praying New Beginnings

The first quarter of Leviticus describes various types of sacrifices or "offerings": "burnt" (chapter 1), "grain" (2), "well-being" (3), "sin" (4), and "guilt" (5), along with a personnel manual for priests in supervising the offerings (6-7). Chapter 1 itself details three kinds of "burnt offerings": "bulls," "sheep/goats," and "birds." Apparently, the first thing Israel needs to get straight on her journey with God through the wilderness is how to sacrifice well!

Much of Leviticus is about what happens on God's side of the sacrifice equation. Namely, it is a matter of "atonement" (v. 4), restoring God and people to a state of "at-one-ment." But it is no accident that when the people of God are given their initial instructions about how to live well with God on a journey, they are taught precisely and elaborately about how to make offerings.

Often, the leader is the most generous person in the room. The leader so treasures well-being (with God, within the holy community, and between the holy community and its surroundings) that s/he will give generously, sacrificially to attain and maintain that. If you aspire to leadership, then your first step today, as with Leviticus, is to learn to be inventively sacrificial.

Exercise: *As you look ahead to your day or week, what is one situation in which you can be the most generous person in the room? Begin to build a muscle for this. Ask God to give you imagination for how to be sacrificial and how to make offerings that reconcile.*

MOTIVE MATTERS

"You shall bring to the Lord the grain offering that is prepared in any of these ways; and when it is presented to the priest, he shall take it to the altar." – Leviticus 2:8

In the "manual of sacrifice" (chapters 1-7), Leviticus 2 describes "*grain offerings.*" These spontaneous acts of worship express gratitude. They include a list of do's and don'ts because worshiping the God of Israel is not to be confused with other forms of deity-worship.

There are at least three noteworthy features of a *"grain offering:"*

1. The sacrifice comes from what feeds people, reminding us that everyday provision of food is a gift from God. Jesus

would thus later teach us to pray, *"Give us this day our daily bread"* (Matthew 6:11).

2. One function of bringing the offering to the altar was to feed and sustain the priests: *"what is left of the grain offering shall be for Aaron and his sons; it is a most holy part of the offerings by fire to the Lord"* (v. 10). Those who mediate the presence of God to the congregation have a right to be fed by the offerings. Paul would later confirm this: *"If we have sown spiritual good among you, is it too much if we reap your material benefits?"* (1 Corinthians 9:11).

3. The key phrase, repeated nine times in chapter 2 (vv. 2f, 8-12, 14, 16) is <u>*"to the Lord."*</u> Offerings are not a meal for the deity. They are not to run a religious business. They are not for the (self) promotion of the giver. They are a gift to the God from whom all provision flows. Thus the prayer I've heard a thousand times in churches when the offering is given: "Lord, we return to you a portion of what is rightfully yours."

Leviticus meticulously explains the external, mechanical details of how to give a good offering. Chapter 3 celebrates the community building that happens when we sacrifice. But as important as these aspects are, they highlight that motive matters. The offering finally affects the offer-er. When we give a sacrificial offering *"to the <u>Lord</u>,"* something very *"pleasing"* (v. 2) to God happens within us.

Exercise: *Meditate on Paul's words in Ephesians 6:7-8: "Render service with enthusiasm, as to the Lord and not to men and women, knowing that whatever good we do, we will receive the same again from the Lord." Ask God to show you some way that you can give or serve today not for personal credit or even primarily for the benefit of another, but as an act of offering worship to God.*

John P. Chandler   193

Leviticus 4-6

MOTIVE DOESN'T MATTER

"If any of you sin without knowing it, doing any of the things that by the Lord's commandments ought not to be done, you have incurred guilt, and are subject to punishment. You shall bring to the priest a ram without blemish from the flock, or the equivalent, as a guilt offering; and the priest shall make atonement on your behalf for the error that you committed unintentionally, and you shall be forgiven." – Leviticus 5:17-18

Leviticus 4-6 lists case studies for what to do in the case of unintentional sin. (There are no provisions for restoring a deliberate sinner.) Various sacrifices of repentance restore the broken vertical link between a person/congregation and God, and they reconcile horizontal disruptions of community life. The pattern in each type of sacrifice is:

Sin *(acknowledgement, sorrow, confession)* → **Blood** *(costly sacrifice)* → **Priest** *(intermediary)* → **Altar** → **God** *(forgives)* → **Restoration** *(vertical and horizontal)*

Later, the New Testament book of Hebrews would build on this thinking by describing how Jesus dealt with our <u>sin</u> through the <u>blood</u> of his cross (<u>altar</u>), acting as a <u>priest</u> on our behalf, making <u>restoration</u> for our <u>sin</u>.

The level of detail about how to make the sacrifices indicates just how serious it is to be out of whack with God. These instructions are for *"the error that you have committed unintentionally."* Ignorance is no defense. If you have gotten out of step with God (and thus the community), an urgent, costly sacrifice done just right is in order. God help you if you have sinned deliberately.

This may sound quaint, ancient, tribal and irrelevant. But what are the costs today when a leader is negligent? Inattentive? Has a failure of nerve? Inadvertently neglects or rashly acts in a way that harms the community in an accidental but very damaging way?

Where Leviticus 2-3 illustrate that motive matters, chapters 4-6 show that motive doesn't matter. Sin is sin whether we intended it or not. It is deadly and contagious, like a disease. It must be dealt with swiftly and properly. Don't waste too much time assigning blame. A leader today knows to fix what's wrong regardless of how it got to be wrong.

Exercise: *Are there things in your relationship with God or with the community you have unintentionally damaged that remain unfixed? If so, end your internal dialogue about whether you "meant" to do it or not. Begin in its place a process of sacrificial restoration to make it right.*

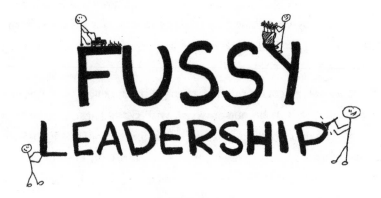

"A perpetual fire shall be kept burning on the altar; it shall not go out." – Leviticus 6:13

Most scholars think that Leviticus was written after Israel's Exile from Babylon, when the people were without land, temple, and nationhood. The people of God lived as resident aliens, minorities within a larger culture that held competing and sometimes hostile values.

Such a context helps us to understand the incredibly fussy level of detail about liturgy, sacrifice, calendar, and priestly regulations in Leviticus. When you aren't the dominant force in your culture, you have to reinforce your identity with different landmarks. For Israel, it was the particular way in which it worshipped and offered sacrifices.

The *"perpetual fire"* is a symbolic reminder of the never-ceasing presence of God in the midst of the community's life. Sacrifice and worship are the center of the community. There is great care and attention to detail in these matters, rather than casual sloppiness, because worship is at the heart of the well-being of people whose lives are centered in God. As Richard Foster writes,

> *"We might think of the image of the actor or musician who practices unceasingly and attends to minute details to give great and lively concerts. So too the careful preparation of congregation and worship leaders, as is witnessed in Leviticus 1-7, helps to facilitate the genuine worship of God, the empowering of the divine-human encounter."*

In our culture, leadership is often talked about as "big-picture" thinking, vision-casting, and remembering to see the forest rather than getting lost in the trees of details. But a good leader can take a cue from Leviticus. When it comes to matters of our core identity, you better get it right. "Close enough" is not good enough. Cross your "t's," dot your "i's," don't be sloppy, attend to the fussy details.

Exercise: *Is there a critical pending decision you need to think and pray through thoroughly before you act on it? Write down accurately the critical details that need attention. Refine and clarify them in conversation with a friend or two. Pray over them. Get the fussy details right with precision, and only then move on the decision.*

HELPING PEOPLE
GET IT RIGHT

"You shall remain at the entrance of the tent of meeting day and night for seven days, keeping the Lord's charge so that you do not die ....." **– Leviticus 8:35**

It is easy to misread the significance of ritual details in Leviticus. They may appear to us to be a monotonous compilation of ancient relics. Or they may come off as legalistic requirements from an obsessive and hostile deity.

But that is easy to say when you are affluent and powerful people who live comfortably as part of majority cultures. When you are a minority people, potentially swallowed or absorbed by a massive society, you have to work hard to remember who you are. Thus what you eat (kosher), how you dress (priestly garments), how you order your calendar (festivals), and how you worship (sacrifices) … these are not casual matters that one can handle roughly. An electrical engineer designs circuits *this way* because it is going to carry current; an architect orders the bridge to be built *just so* because it will bear weight. So also, the *"anointing"* and *"ordination"* (vv. 1, 22) of priestly leaders is to ensure that Israel gets it right when it comes to worship. The risk is real. You "*(keep) the Lord's charge so that you do not die.*"

As minority people, Israel cannot afford the costs of apostasy, compromise, and contamination. Their diet can't be "a little impure," nor can their sacrificial worship be "a little bit off." Ordained leaders dress a certain way, speak a certain way, lead certain rituals because they and their people need to get it right. *Exactly* right. There is serious potency to the presence of God and only fools trifle with that.

Leaders may be ordained not just so they can be "set apart." They help their people be set apart from their surroundings, different in their whole-hearted dedication to the God who can bless.

Exercise: *Is there is an area of your life that is more clean than not, but needs to be totally clean? Reflect on that. After praying, take steps to make (with God's help) this area completely clean. From that experience, look for ways to help others do the same.*

Leviticus 10

REFLECTING GOD or gODS?

"Then Moses said to Aaron, "This is what the Lord meant when he said, "Through those who are near me I will show myself holy, and before all the people I will be glorified."
– Leviticus 10:3

After the "ordination" chapters (Leviticus 8-9), comes this scary episode in chapter 10. *"Aaron's sons, Nadab and Abihu,"* fool around with the priestly offering. Their *"unholy fire"* is met by *"fire (that) came out from the presence of the Lord and consumed them, and they died before the Lord"* (vv. 1-2).

Praying New Beginnings

It seems a little like getting the death penalty for jaywalking ... until you interpret *"unholy"* as "alien." Ritual unholiness connotes ingratitude or even open rebellion against God. These leaders defiantly imported idolatrous practices from other cults into worship. God's reaction was swift and decisive. Would God be offended today if leaders raised a Nazi flag in a worship service and the leaders urged us to sing praise to it? You heard it first in Leviticus!

Nadab and Abihu's demise will be mirrored in the New Testament by the deaths of Ananias and Sapphira at another unholy offering (Acts 5). Both startling episodes demonstrate the power of God's holy presence and our need to fear that potency and regard it with precision and seriousness. What people see their leaders doing shapes their view of God. Moses told Aaron that leaders who are *"near"* God are a vehicle through which God's holiness and *"glory"* is revealed. Or they are not. You simply can't distort that holiness without consequence.

Leaders cannot baptize whatever is popular around them in culture and try to fold it into the worship of almighty God. We who have influence on other people cannot be culturally polluted or corrupted, because what others will see in us shapes who they see God to be.

Exercise: *In what sense do those whom you influence form their view of God by taking their cues from your life? What is one way you can be careful today not to import and reflect unthinkingly some of our cultural gods into your faith and worship?*

DISTINGUISHING AND TEACHING

"You are to distinguishing between the holy and the common, and between the unclean and the clean; and you are to teach the people of Israel all the statues that the Lord has spoken to them through Moses."
– Leviticus 10:10-11

"For I am the Lord who brought you up from the land of Egypt, to be your God; you shall be holy, for I am holy."
– Leviticus 11:45

"Thus you shall keep the people of Israel separate from their uncleanness, so that they do not die in their uncleanness by defiling my tabernacle that is in their midst." – Leviticus 15:31

The heart of Leviticus 10-15 is found in these verses about the work of the leader to *"distinguish"* (between *"holy/common,"* and *"clean/unclean"*), and to *"teach the people"* about this. What follows are long instructions about doing so in regard to animals (chapter 11), bodily cycles (12), and health and sickness (13-15).

Some of the instruction is gross to our sensibilities. Some of it seems arcane. But what is clear is that these nitty-gritty distinctions are about keeping people fit for worship and inclusion in the community whose life is built around God. *That* is a big deal — especially when you are strangers in a strange land. Anomaly is a problem when community is the premium. Being *"unclean"* makes you unfit for worship and community, and so careful attention to such fitness is the work of the spiritual leader. These are not random taboos, but reflections of a covenant of holiness between people and God. God continues his work of ordering chaos into creation through such work.

Spiritual leaders don't lead "off the cuff" and re-mix casually. They watch for community boundaries with discipline, preparation, and not-a-little fear. They guard clear taboos. Failure to do so can be as swift and decisive as exclusion from the community, or even death (10:1ff). They *"distinguish"* and *"teach"* covenant boundaries well, because being included in community with God and others is a matter of life and death. Cleanness, purity, inclusion, wholeness, and health — the presence of God and communion with God's people touches upon every ordinary aspect of our bodily and community life.

Exercise: *What are some fuzzy boundaries within or around your life that need focusing, clarifying, or tightening up? How might God be calling you to respond by* <u>distinguishing</u> *and* <u>teaching</u> *right from wrong or clean from unclean in these instances? Practice today in at least one instance this clarifying work.*

John P. Chandler 203

RESTORATION
THROUGH
SACRIFICE

"For on this day atonement shall be made for you, to cleanse you; from all your sins you shall be clean before the Lord ....This shall be an everlasting statute for you, to make atonement for the people of Israel once in the year for all their sins." – Leviticus 16:30, 34

Praying New Beginnings

In this story, we find some of the central themes of the Bible:

- God's desire for us to be whole and clean in our relationship with him and with the community of those who love him;
- The destructive contaminating power of sin to break those communions;
- The need for decisive intervention to put "at one" (to atone) in order to restore all-important relationship; and
- The gracious gift of God to provide a path for this restoration or "*atonement.*"

Even today, the Jewish people celebrate Yom Kippur, the Day of Atonement from Leviticus 16, remembering the scapegoat sent into *"the wilderness"* to bear *"all the iniquities of the people ... all their iniquities, all their sins"* (vv. 21f). Restoration happens through sacrifice, and the God of the Bible is gracious to provide a path to that wholeness.

The great news of the gospel is that God has provided restoration through the *"the offering of the body of Jesus Christ once for all"* (Hebrews 10:10). The sacrificial work of Jesus on the cross and vindication of his way through the resurrection are God's gift of restoration to all who accept that gift given to them.

Leaders who follow in the way of Jesus are thus marked by the beliefs that a). Restoration is paramount; b). It happens through sacrifice; and c). God is gracious to provide. Following in the path of Jesus, spiritual leaders are restorers, and we restore through the way of sacrifice.

Exercise: *Meditate on the sacrifice of Jesus as God's loving gift of restoration to you. Give humble thanks for it. Ask God to show you a way today to work toward restoring something that is broken, and doing so through the path of sacrifice.*

YOU ARE WHAT YOU EAT

"If anyone of the house of Israel or of the aliens who reside among them eats any blood, I will set my face against the person who eats blood, and will cut that person off from the people. For the life of the flesh is in the blood ...." – Leviticus 17:10-11

While European scholarship of the last two hundred years largely dismissed Leviticus as dealing only with obscure and obsolete ritual matters, scholars more recently have begun to appreciate its thorough connection between the ritual, ethical, and communal. How you carry out ritual determines how you act in the world, and whether you are able to form a community that has a distinct witness that reflects the image of God to the world.

One of the chief ways this happens is through our eating. Leviticus 17 contains five instructions about how to eat well vis-à-vis *"blood."* The people of God don't ingest carelessly or consume randomly. We are more than simply physical beings with bodily needs. We are people who live within the larger creation with the responsibility to bear witness, and eating gives us multiple opportunities to reflect our unique role. It is for no small reason that gluttony is one of the church's seven deadly sins. To eat properly is to reflect well the glory of God. To eat poorly is to disregard holiness.

Samuel Balentine says, "The rituals of holy worship are not only inextricably wedded to the ethics of holy living; they are also fundamentally *generative* of the community's motivation to obedience … Fidelity to ritual has the capacity to *create* ethical sensitivity" (pp. 142f).

Keeping kosher helped Israel to remember its identity. The leader who eats well today regularly remembers and reflects that s/he is a witness, an ethically responsible citizen in the larger creation.

Exercise: *Think spiritually today about what you are eating. How can your intake reflect who God is calling you to be? Forgetting cultural notions of body image or dieting, meditate on how what you consume impacts your witness. Practice asking God to make you mindful of this with each bite you take today.*

John P. Chandler

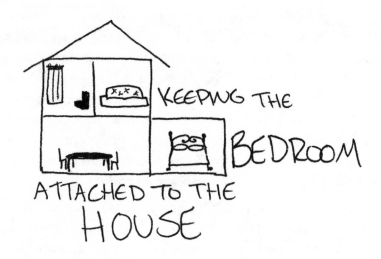

KEEPING THE BEDROOM ATTACHED TO THE HOUSE

"You shall not do as they do in the land of Egypt, where you lived, and you shall not do as they do in the land of Canaan, to which I am bringing you. You shall not follow their statutes." – Leviticus 18:3

Praying New Beginnings

Between the former slavery of Egypt and coming temptation of Canaan lies a way of holiness for Israel. It is the life-giving way (v. 5) to which the people of God are called.

This way includes our sexuality. The faith of Israel keeps the bedroom attached to the house. Israel unblinkingly records bad memories of sexual enslavement and temptation – Abraham and Sarah, Sodom and Gomorrah, Judah and Tamar, Reuben and Bilhah (Genesis 20, 28, 38, and 35). Leviticus 18 similarly warns about the impact of bad sexuality on spirituality with seven warnings not to behave like those who serve other gods (v. 3 twice, vv. 24-30). These are not picky, puritan, or arbitrary taboos. They are rather markers of fidelity and identity. Ritual purity is always mirrored in ethical conduct – including and especially in sexuality. You cannot *"uncover nakedness"* (v. 6, a euphemism for intercourse) in non-covenantal ways and experience the Promised Land life of God. Bad sex destroys the person, family, community, and ultimately *"defiles"* the land (vv. 24ff).

A leader's sex life is not simply his or her personal business. Our sexuality is always tied into our spirituality. Spirituality is always communal. And the community of the people of God is to take its cues neither from past enslavement nor present/future temptation, but from its covenantal identity that mirrors life-giving holiness. What we do in bed is attached to the rest of the house.

Exercise: *In your own sexuality, is past enslavement or present/future temptation more of a threat to your identity? If enslavement, ask God to grant you forgiveness, release, and liberation. If temptation, ask God for strength, clarity, perseverance, and true community. In all things, pray that God would make you faithful sexually so that you can lead communally.*

John P. Chandler 209

Leviticus 19

HOLY LEADERSHIP

"You shall be holy, for I the Lord your God am holy."
– Leviticus 19:2

This is the signature line of all of Leviticus. It is the keynote of chapters 17-26, the "Holiness Code." And it is the centerpiece for helping the people of God to understand that the ritual is always tied up with the ethical.

Holiness is the idea that our inner life with God will form the wellspring of our life in key relationships with others. There is a fundamental movement of "Up-In-Out" in chapter 19:

- Verses 1-8 speak of obligations "<u>up</u>" to God in worship: *"Do not turn to idols or make cast images for yourselves; I am the Lord your God"* (v. 4);

- Verses 9-18 list requirements "<u>in</u>" toward fellow community members: *"You shall love your neighbor as yourself; I am the Lord your God"* (v. 18);

- Verses 19-37 detail practices of holy people within the larger *"alien"* civilization: *"You shall keep all my statutes and all my ordinances, and observe them: I am the Lord"* (v. 37).

Unthinking modern passersby miss the profound point when they simply dismiss the whole by mocking particular now-obsolete regulations (such as prohibiting mixed garments in v. 19). Rabbi Joshua Heschel says,

> *"If a man is not more than human then he is less than human. Judaism is an attempt to prove that in order to be a man, you have to be more than a man, that in order to be a people we have to be more than a people. Israel was made to be a holy people."* (Heschel, *I Asked for Wonder*, quoted in Balentine, p. 150).

Holiness means that <u>worship</u> or <u>ritual</u> ("Up") is the foundation for ethical <u>community</u> ("In"), which forms the basis for <u>witness</u> ("Out") into the alien world. Holiness is about an integrated life capable of blessing the world. It flows from the identity of God (*"I am the Lord"*).

A leader in the Leviticus holiness tradition will audit her or his "Up-In-Out" integration. It forms distinctiveness worth following.

Exercise: *Do a personal "Up-In-Out" audit. Which of the three should be your primary focus for today, this week, and this season of life? Mark a note on your calendar for the end of the day, end of the week, and end of the quarter to review how this has gone.*

THE STUFF THAT WILL MAKE YOU SICK

*"You shall keep all of my statutes and all my ordinances,
and observe them, so that the land to which I bring you to
settle in may not vomit you out. You shall not follow the
practices of the nation that I am driving out before you.
Because they did all these things, I abhorred them."*
– Leviticus 20:22-23

Because it duplicates warnings found in previous chapters (18-19) of the Holiness Code, Leviticus 20 often receives little more than a glance. As case law, it spells out specific offenses so that there is no doubt about how the people of God are to set themselves apart from the larger national context. Israel is different and *"shall not follow the practices of the nation."* If she "goes along to get along," the consequence will be violent expulsion from the land: God will *"vomit you out."*

What is the stuff that will make the people of God sick? Chapter 20 outlines four main categories:

1. <u>Child sacrifice</u> (vv. 2-6) – the practice (for religious or economic reasons) of giving *"their offspring to Molech,"* the national god. When people sacrifice their children on the altar of well-being as defined by the nation, it profanes God's name.

2. <u>Bad religion</u> (vv. 6ff, 27) – occult or superstition. The primary outcome of living this way is family brokenness (v. 9).

3. <u>Sexual perversion</u> (vv. 10-21) – primarily listed in categories of incest, homosexuality, bestiality. Described also as *"abomination"* (v. 13), *"depravity"* (14), *"disgrace"* (17), and *"impurity"* (21), the outcomes for bad sexual practice range from death to barrenness. The largest category describes a state of breakdown in community: *"they shall be cut off in the sight of their people"* (v. 17).

4. <u>Unclean eating</u> (vv. 25f) – you are what you eat, and the people are God are to be a witness to the larger context about how they consume.

Suddenly Leviticus doesn't look so obscure to contemporary leadership and decision-making. What are guidelines for setting us apart (in a good way) as holy leaders today? Treat your children right. Don't live superstitiously. Be pure sexually. Watch what you eat. Doing poorly in any of these areas can vomit us out of holy influence. But if we make good decisions in these arenas, then we have a chance to bear God's witness to our larger community.

Exercise: *Take stock of the four categories in your life: children, superstition, your sexuality, and your consumer habits. Rate yourself from one (struggling) to ten (thriving) in each area. What is God saying to you about how you are doing in each category?*

John P. Chandler

"The priest who is exalted above his fellows, on whose head the anointing oil has been poured and who has been consecrated to wear the vestments, shall not dishevel his hair, nor tear his vestments." – Leviticus 21:10

To be "holy" means to be set apart for special service. The call to holiness is for the whole people of God. Israel was to be a unique witness within Canaan. The church is to be set apart from the world in order to bless the world. And in Leviticus 21-22, the priestly leaders within the people of God are set apart as holy in order to model and exemplify holiness to others.

Because of this role, there are special rules for priests. These leaders are governed not only by the general practices of holiness that apply to all the people. Rather, their visibility and role means they also live by a code that takes special care to guard the mission of the people.

Thus there are special rules for leaders about what events they attend (21:1ff), whom they marry (v. 7ff), what they give (22:1ff), and even their appearance (21:10ff). There is to be no mix-up. The leader is not like everyone else. They are set apart in visible ways in order to demonstrate as a living example how the rest of the people are to be set apart. They don't dress (*"vestments"*) like everyone else nor style (*"dishevel their hair"*) like everyone else. They are not like everyone else. They are an example for everyone else.

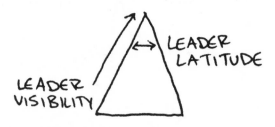

The more visibility leaders have, the less "side-to-side" behavioral latitude we have. The higher we climb in our modeling roles, the more tightly defined are the limits of what is acceptable and good. That narrowing can feel restrictive, but is ultimately clarifying. What we lose in open options, we gain in focus. The leader can rise to the level that s/he is willing to live by a higher standard than the general public.

Exercise: *What are some "special rules" that you need to keep which don't apply to the general public? Given your influence, is there anything you need to tighten up on in your behavior, attendance, and appearance?*

Leviticus 23

"These are the appointed festivals of the Lord that you shall proclaim as holy convocations, my appointed festivals." – Leviticus 23:2

When you live in a land that is not your own, one of the ways you can clarify your identity is through determining your calendar. If you can't re-shape the <u>space</u> around you, then you can re-form your <u>time</u>.

Leviticus 23 does this by listing the major feast days that Israel is to observe: Passover, first fruits, Pentecost, the Day of Atonement, and the feast of booths. These are *"holy convocations"* or *"appointed festivals,"* times when Israel is repeatedly and strongly warned not to *"work at your occupations"* (vv. 7f, 21, 25, 28, 30ff, 35f). Like the weekly *"sabbath"* (v. 3), the severest punishments are for those who do not stop working at their normal jobs.

The weekly day of sabbath and seasonal festivals thus mark Israel as distinct from people around them. Sabbath and festivals are "finish lines" which mark time in commemoration with the acts of God in Israel's life rather than in natural phenomena like the change of seasons. As festivals, they were eagerly awaited. Yet, the temptation to skip them for work must have been powerful, so the warnings to cease working in order to celebrate were loud and clear.

We need finish lines. We need times on the calendar that mark the completion of something and the time to begin something else. Intuitively, we know to mark time like birthday celebrations. But a spiritual leader will be intentional and rigorous about naming and keeping finish lines. These are times to stop working, mark time, celebrate, give an offering, and be thankful. Without them, we work ourselves to death.

Exercise: *Think day, week, and season. What is a finish line you need to observe in each unit of time? When you discern these finish lines, physically mark them in your calendar. As you observe them, note what happens in your heart. And when you have completed them, put a checkmark by them on the calendar – and give thanks to God for sabbath and festivals.*

Leviticus 24

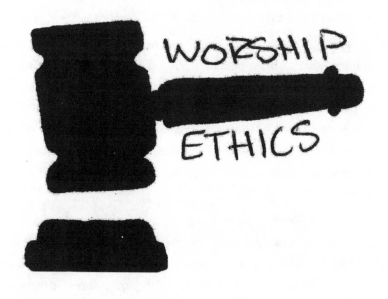

"And they put him into custody, until the decision of the Lord should be made clear to them." – Leviticus 24:12

This chapter centers on a story where the people of God have to decide how to handle a case of blasphemy. In the heat of a fight within the community, a young man *"blasphemed the Name in a curse"*

Praying New Beginnings

(v. 11). To their credit, the community did not immediately lash out in retribution. They rather entered into a period of deliberation and discernment *"until the decision of the Lord should be made clear to them."*

The frame around the incident illumines how the community made the decision to execute the man. The first part of the chapter is about proper worship, particularly the perpetually burning *"lamp"* and regular *"offering"* (vv. 1-9). The back end of the chapter is about the larger code of *"eye for eye, tooth for tooth"* legal ethics (vv. 15-23). This *"one law for the alien and for the citizen"* (v. 22) was a legal and humanitarian advance that limited retribution equitably. It was an ethical step forward in ancient civilization to curb ever-escalating honor retaliation. The punishment must fit the crime proportionately.

The structure of the chapter gives the moral of the story: proper worship leads to ethical legal decision-making. When we are worshipers, we don't simply strike back in anger at wrongdoers. Rather, we deliberate, and we lean toward equitable justice.

Leaders learn to curb emotional retaliation. At our best, we choose to respond to a serious offense by entering into a period of discernment, at which time we think about justice in light of who we are as a worshiping community. Justice may be fierce, but it will never be an impulsive strike-back.

Exercise: *Are you facing a decision that evokes great emotion from you? If so, how can you take a step back from an immediate response, enter into a period of discernment, and respond out of who you are as an ethical worshiper? What is a practical way that you can delay until you are able to discern?*

RELEASING POSESSIONS

"And you shall hallow the fiftieth year and you shall proclaim liberty throughout the land to all its inhabitants. It shall be a jubilee for you: you shall return, every one of you, to your property and every one of you to your family." – Leviticus 25:10

If the bell closing Wall Street is the great symbol of our nation's economy ("whoever accumulates the most at the end of the day wins"), then the trumpet of Jubilee is to be the sounding symbol for the people of God. Every fiftieth year, when this trumpet blows, there is to be a great restart. All property returns to its original owner. All cycles of accumulation, of haves and have-nots, are rebooted. All of society together remembers that God owns everything. We are not the owners. We are stewards of possessions. We are resident aliens who tend the property owned ultimately by God.

This Jubilee trumpet is how God defines community. As Walter Brueggemann says, "Life in the community of faith does not consist getting more but in sharing well." Jubilee is the electrical shock that restores sanity. It is a scheduled reboot that periodically reminds us that the ceaseless pursuit of acquisition does not make for life. You must give back what was never really yours in the first place if you want to live.

Leaders are often rewarded with possessions for their work. This pattern can be very seductive. We can begin to believe that the better we are as leaders, the more we will own. Leviticus 25 reminds us that this is a lie. It actually runs in the opposite direction of neighborliness and true community. Our money, our land, our possessions are not really ours. They are to be like our children. As such, we are to hold them lightly, take care of them … and be ready to let them go.

Exercise: *Do you have any possessions that are getting in the way of your full obedience to God and true experience of community or neighborliness? If so, write down a few of them. Ask God to show you what releasing these things would look like. Pray for the ability to open any clenched hands, and to hold on loosely or even fully release anything that is interfering with what makes for true joy in your life.*

John P. Chandler 221

ENVIRONMENTAL CONSEQUENCES

"I will break your proud glory, and I will make your sky like iron and your earth like copper. Your strength shall be spent to no purpose: your land shall not yield its produce, and the trees of the land shall not yield their fruit."
– Leviticus 26:19-20

Chapter 26 concludes the "Holiness Code" (Leviticus 17-26). It is the book's final statement about what will make the people of God distinct from the world in order to bless the world. Like other Old Testament summary statements (Exodus 23, Deuteronomy 28, Joshua 24, Psalm 1), Leviticus 26 lays out "the two ways." At the end of the day, the Holiness Code presents stark alternatives. While there are gray areas for interpreting specific cases, at the end of it all, there is truly a black and white choice: either to follow obediently the God who delivered you from slavery in order to be distinct. Or don't.

What makes Leviticus 26 unique is its focus on the environmental consequences that inevitably follow that fundamental choice of (dis)obedience. Most of the rewards for faithful following are descriptions of *"peace in the land"* (v. 6), including the absence of *"dangerous animals"* and presence of abundance of harvest (vv. 6, 10). On the other hand, many of the punishments for God's people failing to live distinctively detail *"land that lies desolate"* (vv. 34f). The *"proud glory"* of disobedient people results in a *"sky like iron"* and *"earth like copper"* – metallic, unfruitful, unnatural, and polluted.

The great lie of individualism in the United States is that our choices are our own business alone. Leviticus 26, like the rest of the Bible, scoffs at such foolishness. Our decisions as leaders impact the environment around us, for good or ill. The consequences of the path we take extend far beyond what we touch directly. We never lead in a vacuum. The very "field" around us is seeded or poisoned by the pathway we choose.

Exercise: *Evaluate the "environment" in which you lead. Is the atmosphere around you vibrant or polluted, fruitful or barren? In what ways does that the larger environment around you reflect leadership choices you or others have made? What might God be calling you to learn and do about that?*

John P. Chandler 223

Leviticus 27

"... the priest shall compute for it the proportionate assessment up to the year of jubilee, and the assessment shall be paid as of that day, a sacred donation to the Lord." – Leviticus 27:23

Just when Leviticus seemed to peak at the end of the Holiness Code (chapters 17-26), chapter 27 comes as an appendix dealing with religious vows. Apparently, the last word of Leviticus is that keeping your promises is kind of important to the life of holiness!

There are all kinds of things that can be devoted or dedicated to God through sacred vows:

Praying New Beginnings

- Persons (vv. 1-8)
- Animals (9-13)
- Buildings (14f)
- Land (16-25)
- Firstlings (26f)
- Devoted things (28f)
- Tithes (30-33)

This fits in with the overall aim of Leviticus: to help the people of God pay careful attention to all of the ordinary stuff of life. We are to live methodically and intentionally. We consecrate all of our personal and communal habits as the stuff of holiness. Even how we deal with animals and fields becomes part of our worship and witness. And particularly when we make vows, the final word of Leviticus is that our promises will be watched carefully – so make them judiciously and keep them scrupulously.

A leader who wants to be holy will sometimes draw attention to the seriousness and importance of something by making a vow concerning it. S/he will then be held accountable to fulfill that promise. Wise is the leader who understands that ordinary things belong to God, who makes careful promises, and then follows through on keeping them.

Exercise: *Looking at the above list about the types of things that can be intentionally dedicated to God, do any of them call for a vow from you? What promise(s) might you make? Don't decide quickly! Meditate and deliberate until you have a clear sense of call from God about this promise. When you do, tell it to a holy person, and ask them to hold you accountable to fulfill your vow.*

LEARNING TO COUNT

*"The Lord spoke to Moses in the wilderness of Sinai,
in the ten of meeting, on the first day of the second
month, in the second year after they had come out of
the land of Egypt, saying: "Take a census of the whole
congregation...."* – Numbers 1:1-2

The English title of the book of Numbers comes from Greek and Latin words derived from the census in chapters 1-4 and 26. The Hebrew Bible instead calls the book, "In the Wilderness." Both titles capture core ideas. This part of the story is about learning to leave the security of familiar slavery and travel in wilderness places toward new freedoms. It is also about learning to number, count, and to bring structure to confusion.

The story begins with the words, "*The Lord spoke to Moses.*" God's first command, echoing his own work at the Genesis 1 creation of all things, is for Moses the leader to number the innumerable and to bring order to chaos. Just as Leviticus wants to help God's people understand "clean and unclean," so Numbers wants to help us deal with boundaries. Who belongs to what tribe? Who has what responsibility? How do we, in our new freedoms, learn to discipline ourselves to meet new tests? Like children becoming teenagers, the people of God have to learn these tasks in the wilderness, on a journey, through much testing. And they begin their learning by numbering.

It's not sexy, but an early part of growing up in spirituality and leadership involves learning to count. It is an acquired skill. Leaders first have to learn to listen to what the Lord speaks. Then, often, the next assignment is about how to count, what to count, and how to assign boundaries. Observing boundaries and learning to count are skills acquired early on. Without them, we never make disciplined decisions as free people, and we don't journey well.

Exercise: *What is something God is asking you to "number" or count right now? Why so? What is God trying to form in you by asking you to quantify this? Make a plan to start counting.*

John P. Chandler   227

Numbers 2

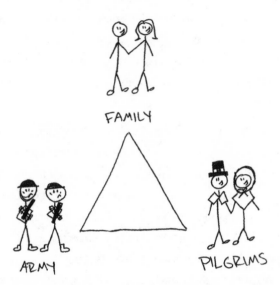

FAMILY

ARMY

PILGRIMS

"The Lord spoke to Moses and Aaron, saying: The Israelites shall camp each in their respective regiments under ensigns by their ancestral houses; they shall camp facing the tent of meeting on every side."
– Numbers 2:1-2

When Israel first escaped slavery in Egypt, they did so with great urgency and very little organization. But now, as they begin a long march through the wilderness, what they need is order, structure, and discipline. Urgency and disciplined order – both are necessary in life with God, each waxing and waning with specific seasons on the journey.

Numbers 2 describes the organization of the people of God as a symmetrical design around the *"tent of meeting"* or dwelling place where Moses met the Lord among the people. It gives three core metaphors for how the people are organized: by family (*"ancestral*

Praying New Beginnings

houses"), as an <u>army</u> ("*regiments, ensigns, companies*"), and as <u>pilgrims</u> (a congregation arranged around the presence of God, on journey with God toward the Promised Land). Each metaphor gives a valid clue to identity and to how God's people function.

Today, just as Moses did, leaders can call on people to put on different "hats." Are we to think of ourselves now as <u>family</u>? If so, our premiums are on loving relationships. Or are we an <u>army</u> right now? If so, our premium is not on loving relationships but to be well-oiled platoon to "take that hill." Or, are we right now <u>pilgrims</u> together, a congregation in the business of being centered around God and on a sacred and dangerous journey together? Here's another way to think about it – are we:

All are legitimate ways of structuring our life together. The good leader knows when it is time to bring one model or the other to the forefront.

Exercise: *Right now, which metaphor is fitting for you to use as you think about the people you lead or influence – family, army, or pilgrims? How will this image affect the way you interact with those people today? Look to be intentional and clear in what you are aiming for based out of that image.*

"According to the commandment of the Lord through Moses they were appointed to their several tasks of serving or carrying ...." **– Numbers 4:49**

True to its name, the book of Numbers spends a lot of time counting. Smart readers pay attention to what it counts, and why. If you can figure out what to count and why, you can lead!

Numbers 3 and 4 count various priestly lines – the *"Levites"* and their sub-tribes, the *"Kohathites, Gershonites, and Merarites."* Each are carefully *"enrolled"* or *"appointed"* through a *"census"* to have responsibility with *"the most holy things"* (4:4) pertaining to the religious life of the community. Priestly servants were unique reminders who helped Israel remember its unique witness as a minority people in a strange land.

The key *"tasks"* of these set-apart leaders are *"serving or carrying."* There is a lot of tabernacle break-down, toting, and reassembling for a people on the move. Because this *"tent of meeting"* is the central place where Israel maintains its true identity, transportation has to be done with precision and diligence. It's not a sexy job but one that has to be done repeatedly and right. The Bible consistently demonstrates that leaders are lead servants. What counts in biblical leadership is *"serving and carrying."*

Those who follow Jesus as the great and final high priest believe that he has made every one of us to be part of a *"holy priesthood"* (1 Peter 2:5). We are all numbered as priestly servants, not just specially anointed or ordained technicians. If any of us are singled out in unique ways, it is to highlight how we do the work of *"serving and carrying."* We are called to lead inasmuch as we are lead servants. That's what deserves counting.

Exercise: *In what way do you need to serve or carry today or this week? How are you going to "count" whether you did that well or poorly? Ask God for the strength and focus to be humble, persistent, and consistent. And ask for wisdom to "count" well.*

Numbers 5

"… they must not defile their camp, where I dwell among them." – Numbers 5:3

This chapter, frankly, is an example of how and why the Bible needs "landscaping" in order to be read and applied well for leadership in our day. It is clearly patriarchal and is most infamous for its use in the 1692 Salem witch hunts. These trials by ordeal resulted in unjust deaths for many women, and a terrible reputation for the puritans who executed them. If anything, (mis)application of Numbers 5 became the American example of what harm follows from hysterical religious extremism. One early observer said that the Salem witch trials by ordeal were "the rock on which theocracy shattered" in colonial America.

Praying New Beginnings

So, when we encounter a Scripture whose meaning has been so widely misapplied that it actually encourages the opposite of what it intends, we either move on to more evidently fruitful biblical territory, or we peel a few more layers back to get to the heart of the hopes within that Scripture.

And what Numbers 5 intends (several layers down!) is the portrait of an undefiled community. The Bible describes this quest in various ways – in terms of holiness, purity, clean vs. unclean. The great and worthy vision behind all of this is God's intention for his people to form a beautiful colony in a wider land. This community is not isolated and weird. It is rather a magnetic example of flourishing through serious and intentional sanctity. In this community, things like lying (vv. 5-10) and adultery (vv. 11ff) are treated not as minor personal offenses. They are serious threats to a vision and mission worth protecting zealously.

So, rather than shrugging off Numbers 5 as an example of why not to take the Bible seriously, allow it to challenge you: what is *your* vision for an undefiled and beautiful community? In that community, how seriously would you treat lying and sexual infidelity?

Exercise: *What might so threaten the witness that God intends for you and those in your tribe that it demands a swift and severe response? How would you respond to that serious threat? How would you answer those who mock your response as a witch hunt? If there is a situation in your life and community like that now, ask God for guidance through it. If one does not exist, allow time to ponder guidelines and principles for how you would hope to respond one day.*

John P. Chandler 233

Numbers 6

THE GREAT BLESSING

*"You shall say to them, The Lord bless you and keep you;
the Lord make his face to shine upon you and be gracious
to you; the Lord lift his countenance upon you, and give
you peace. So they shall put my name upon the Israelites,
and I will bless them." – Numbers 6:23-27*

This is the great and ancient blessing of the Bible, the words pronounced by the priests upon the congregation of God's people as they leave the time and zone set apart for worship. It is a "benediction," a word that "speaks well" over us. It *"puts"* the name of God *"upon"* his people, marking them with the divine character – which is to bless. God's people are blessed in order to be a blessing to the world, just as Abraham was in the beginning (Genesis 12:3).

This blessing cascades and gains momentum, each phrase growing longer than the one before it. Its final word is the great promise of the Bible: *shalom*, the peace and wholeness God hopes for his people and for all of creation. *Shalom* both describes the state of the people of God who have been in worship, and captures our marching orders as we leave a zone of worship to go into a world that decidedly has <u>not</u> been in worship. It prepares us to re-enter that wider world, marked by God, as agents and ambassadors of the shining *"face"* of the holy God.

As Walter Brueggemann puts it, such a benediction is "part promise, part assurance, part hope, part wish, but in fact (it is) the simple truth of the gospel, that God's holy, life-giving presence does not end when we depart each other; it continues amid our several distinct journeys of obedience."

The God who brought Israel out of slavery and raised Jesus from the dead … this God wants to put his name or presence on you, and through you, onto the world. In the words of an old hymn, you and I "take the name of Jesus with you" to mark our new life in the world.

Exercise: *In what ways might the name of Jesus be "upon" me as I go through the day? How might I pass on a blessing to another today, just as I have been blessed? Pray for God to give you the eyes to envision these possibilities.*

John P. Chandler   235

Numbers 7

LEAD GIVERS

"The Lord said to Moses: They shall present their offerings, one leader each day, for the dedication of the altar." – Numbers 7:11

The most striking feature of Numbers 7 is its painstaking description of the offering given by each of the twelve tribal leaders before they marched through the wilderness. In the spirit of those lists, here is a short list of what we learn from it about the correlation of leading and giving:

- The first act of leaders is to bring *"their offerings before the Lord"* (v. 2).

- They give <u>before</u> setting out on the journey (v. 1). They did not give based on results or track record, but in faith and in prophetic anticipation.

- The leaders were united and harmonious in giving. Israel's single vision comes into focus, rather than any tribal divisions.

- The giving is systematic and planned (*"one leader each day*, v. 11), not spontaneous and emotion-driven.

- The offerings were quite public, and the final tally was a big deal (vv. 84-88).

- Perhaps most importantly, at the end of this long focus on the leaders' gifts, Moses was then able to *"speak to the Lord"* and also *"would hear the voice speaking to him"* (v. 89). There was fresh revelation on the heels of the leaders' offering.

Leaders are lead givers. Behind-the-scenes contributions matter, but our public gifts set the context for speaking to and hearing from God. A good and worshipful leader is unafraid to model the way through her or his public example of giving.

Exercise: *Giving is usually a private or personal matter in our culture, and there can be spiritual dangers in "showing off" with loud gifts (see Matthew 6:2-4). Having acknowledged this caution, is there a way that I can set a positive example through a public demonstration of giving? Reflect on how you might show leadership through your public giving.*

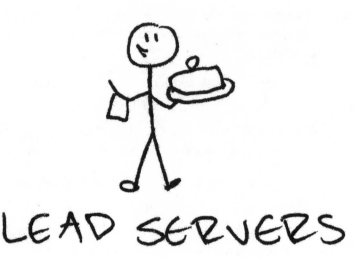

LEAD SERVERS

"When you bring the Levites before the Lord, the Israelites shall lay their hands on the Levites, and Aaron shall present the Levites before the Lord as an elevation offering from the Israelites, that they may do the service of the Lord." – Numbers 8:10-11

Numbers 8 sets apart *"Levites"* as a unique tribe of spiritual leaders. They undergo a consecration ceremony (vv. 5ff, 20-22) of shaving and washing *"to cleanse them"* for *"purification"* (v. 7). Their role in the traveling camp is to shield the rest of the tribe from the *"plague"* (v. 19) that would surely come upon the people were they to treat casually the holy presence of God in their midst. Notice two characteristics about who these leaders <u>are</u>, and two descriptions of what they <u>do</u>. Who they **are:**

- They are an *"elevation offering"* (vv. 11, 13, 15, 21), lifted up to visibility among the people for their spiritual work.

- They are *"unreservedly given"* (v. 16) *"to do duty in the service of the Lord"* (vv. 24-26), complete with a term limit (ages 25-50) and post-duty assignment to *"assist their brothers."* In summary, these leaders are visible, set apart, work for a season, step aside, and are flexible to change roles in the seasons of life.

What these leaders **do**:

- Simply, they *"do service"* (vv. 11, 19, 26). This is simultaneously *"of the Lord"* (v. 11), *"for the Israelites"* (v. 19), and with *"their brothers"* or fellow servants (v. 26).

- This service is to *"make atonement"* (vv. 12, 19), setting things "at one" between God and the people.

In Romans 12, every follower of Jesus is called upon in their baptism to become a *"living sacrifice."* Thus we are all priests, all Levites, all elevated and given in our own context, all given to serve and set things at one. To offer yourself as a living sacrifice is to be a lead servant.

Exercise: *Which of these words is God most bringing to the forefront in your own spiritual leadership today:* **"elevation"** ... **"unreservedly given"** ... **"do service"** ... **"make atonement"**? *Allow time for the Holy Spirit to let these phrases settle into your heart until one of them becomes your assignment for today or for this current season.*

THE VALUE OF AGILITY

"Whether it was two days, or a month, or a longer time, that the cloud continued over the tabernacle, resting upon it, the Israelites would remain in camp and would not set out; but when it lifted they would set out. At the command of the Lord they would camp, and at the command of the Lord they would set out."
– Numbers 9:22-23

Israel has received the clear revelation of God's will at Sinai. They now have clear guidelines of exactly what they are to do in order to be a holy witness and blessing to the world. At the beginning of Numbers 9, they even receive a clarifying ruling on how to proceed with a murky legal interpretation about faithfully keeping the Passover. They are all set to go.

Final instructions before departing are simple. The presence of God is symbolized by *"fire"* by night and *"cloud"* by day. *"Whenever the cloud lifted over the tent"* (or *"tabernacle"*), then the people of God are to *"set out"* on the journey (v. 17). On the other hand, *"where the cloud settled down, there the Israelites would camp."* The time frame was variable and could not be forecasted – overnight, a couple of days, a month, longer. So that there would be no confusion, God told Moses to use clear trumpet blasts *"for summoning the congregation, and for breaking camp"* (10:2).

The people of God don't need a map through the wilderness; they need a guide. They don't need a long-term plan but the ability to hear and respond to living instruction. Short-term responsiveness is more important than long-range forecasting. God is interested not in their powers to initiate or predict, but in whether they would follow his lead, his timing, his cloud.

Henry Blackaby once wisely said that when you are not sure about following the will of God, then "obey the last clear thing you heard God say to you." Keep doing what you are sure God has called you to do until you are sure that God is calling you to do something else.

God is interested in a leader's responsiveness. He values our agility, that is, our ability to stop and rest or pick up and move at a moment's notice, unburdened by forecasts, long-range plans, or predictions. He wants us to trust him as the Planner more than we trust in our own plans.

Exercise: *What is the last clear thing God told you to do? Rather than pining for the next step of your adventure, focus today on your level of obedience to what you currently are certain that God wants from you.*

THE VALUE
OF
SCOUTING

*"Do not leave us, for you know where we should camp in
the wilderness, and you will serve as eyes for us."*
– Numbers 10:31

The *"cloud"* of God's presence has lifted, giving the Israelites the "go" signal for journeying through the wilderness. Singing the "song of the ark" (vv. 35f), Israel marches out, praising the Lord, who is the divine warrior going before them. Nineteen days after the census of 1:1, they are organized and begin to *"set out by stages from the wilderness of Sinai"* (v. 12) on command.

While most of the chapter concerns itself with the processional order, there is an interesting inset about a conversation between Moses and *"Hobab"* (or Jethro), the son of Moses' father-in-law. Promising to *"treat you well"* and to do for him *"whatever good the Lord does for us"* (vv. 29, 32), Moses begs Hobab not to return to Midian but to accompany Israel through the wilderness. Moses believes Hobab will help determine *"where we should camp in the wilderness"* as well as serving *"as eyes for us."* He wants a scout.

Doug Murren said that wise leaders find a few "spies" or "scouts" to work with them. They get people who will both go ahead and simultaneously report advance information that will be useful in decision-making. They can give you "ground truth" about what is out there. Their advance news is not always what we want to hear, but we make better decisions with even unhappy facts than we do with happy fictions or wishful thinking.

If you can find such scouts, take care of them – they are invaluable to you!

Exercise: *Who is someone who can be a "scout" or "spy" for you? What would you want them to do? How can you take care of them well as they serve you and the aims you are trying to accomplish?*

Numbers 11

DEALING WITH WHINING

"So the Lord said to Moses, "Gather for me seventy of the elders of Israel ... I will come down and talk with you there; and I will put some of the spirit that is on you and put it on them; and they shall bear the burden of the people along with you so that you will not bear it all by yourself." – Numbers 11:16-17

Numbers 11 begins a series of stories scholars call the "rebellion narratives." Like teenagers, Israel is hardly into its journey when the whining begins. *"If only we had meat to eat!"* (v. 4). *"Surely it was better for us in Egypt"* (v. 18). Even in the face of miraculous provision of manna (not to mention deliverance from slavery!), there is weeping and complaining so fierce that *"the Lord became very angry, and Moses was displeased"* (v. 10).

There are several responses to the persistent whining of people who ought to be thanking heaven. Some of the responses belong only to God, who alone can decide whether to provide quail, or destroy with plague or fire (vv. 31-35, 1-3).

However, the instruction for Moses as a human leader can be useful for us. God tells Moses to distribute leadership and let the power of the Spirit be exercised through a number of *"elders."* Moses doesn't want to be a solo wet-nurse to infantile people (vv. 11-15), and God doesn't want one person bearing the burden of dealing with rebellious whiners alone. Here, the Lord's power is <u>not</u> limited because leadership is shared. The divine Spirit rests on many prophets and leaders (vv. 23ff).

When you have to deal with people who can never get enough, whose *"craving"* and *"weeping"* and rejection ignore all evidence, one of the best moves you can make as a leader is to bring others alongside of you to share the burden, speak the prophetic word, and distribute the Lord's power. A committee of one is never a good strategy. With distributed leadership, you may still get angry, and people still may get burned for their rebellion. But this is the biblical and sustainable path for dealing with the difficult.

Exercise: *Who is driving you crazy right now? List three wise people who can help you deal with the headache this person is causing you. Make a plan to tap each helper this week, and make notes on your calendar to revisit this situation a week from now, and a month from now.*

"Now the man Moses was very humble, more so than anyone else on the face of the earth." – Numbers 12:3

The rebellion at the edge of the camp (11:1-4) now spreads to the inner circle. Miriam and Aaron, key spokespersons of the tribe, dislike Moses' marrying a foreign (Ethiopian) wife. This becomes the pretext for an attack on his spiritual authority: *"they said, "Has the Lord spoken only through Moses?"*

God hears this character attack and responds in two ways. One, he strikes Miriam with a dread disease (vv. 10ff; but why not Aaron, too?) and Moses has to talk God out of more harsh punishment (vv. 13ff). Second, God uses the episode to clarify to everyone that he has a special and unmediated relationship with Moses: *"With him I speak face to face – clearly, not in riddles; and he beholds the face of the Lord"* (v. 8). God *"entrusts"* Moses with *"all my house"* (v. 7). Moses is a unique spiritual leader – and why? Because Moses was *"very humble, more so than anyone else on the face of the earth."* Moses' meekness qualified him as a leader to the point that God defended him from poisonous jealousy from would-be rivals.

Humility in the leader seems to make one vulnerable to attack from others. It does not angrily and noisily defend itself in the face of accusation. It leans on God for justice rather than seeking retribution when wronged. Like Moses here, and like Jesus to come, it responds to attack with intercession and undeserved kindness.

Meek leadership is the opposite of self-interest and self-preservation. Its reward is unmediated friendship and conversation with God for clarity and guidance.

Exercise: *Is there a leader of whom you are critical right now? Revisit your difficulty with that person; are you in dangerous territory when you make statements about their character based on disagreement over their tactical decisions? Ask God to examine your heart and guard your lips.*

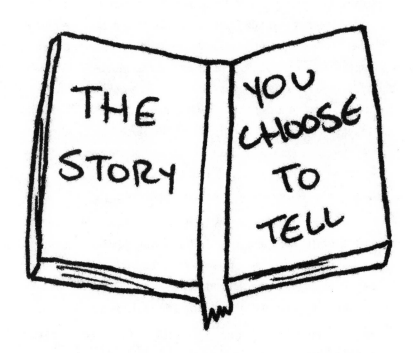

"Moses sent them to spy out the land of Canaan, and said to them ... "Be bold and bring some of the fruit of the land."... "The land that we have tone through as spies is a land that devours its inhabitants; and all the people that we saw in it are of great size ... to ourselves we seemed like grasshoppers." – Numbers 13:17, 20, 32-33

This story illustrates the principle, "What you see is what you get." Undeterred by attacks on his leadership and character in chapter 12, meek Moses continues to lead progressively and boldly. Moses knows the value of advance scouting (see 10:31) and thus sends out twelve spies ahead of the tribe to investigate Canaan.

Moses wants ground truth from Canaan, but he also wants the spies to come back with a report that is in character with his people's divine mandate and calling. He's not looking for spin and untruth, but looking for his spies to bring back a story in keeping with the larger story of what a faithful God is doing. Thus us tells the spies to *"be bold"* and *"bring back some of the fruit of the land."*

Ten of the spies disobey and come back with *"an unfavorable report"* (32), a story of terror. The towns are too *"fortified,"* the people are *"very large,"* and *"we seemed like grasshoppers"* (vv. 28, 33). Only Caleb (and in the next chapter, Joshua) tells a different story: *"Let us go up at once and occupy it, for we are well able to overcome it"* (v. 30). His report is in line with the history of a God who has thus far been able to deliver Israel out of slavery in Egypt and provide for them daily in the wilderness.

My colleague, Kathryn McElveen, teaches young couples that the story they tell about each other is critical to the success of their marriage. A husband and wife can describe each other as "exact opposites" or "perfect complements." The story they choose to tell about each other will be the story they live into.

Great leaders don't spin the facts. But they do choose which story into which they will live.

Exercise: *How are you telling the story of what God is doing through you? Do you need to revisit how you are framing a leadership situation so that it reflects the much larger story of grace and deliverance that you have experienced at the hand of a faithful God? Give some thought to this, and practice re-telling your story with a different framework.*

Numbers 14

WHAT HAPPENS TO WICKED COMPLAINERS

"None of the people who have seen my glory and the signs that I did in Egypt and in the wilderness, and yet have tested me these ten times and have not obeyed my voice, shall see the land that I swore to give to their ancestors; none of those who despised me shall see it."
– Numbers 14:22-23

In underestimating themselves (*"we seemed like grasshoppers,"* 13:33) and overestimating the Canaanites (*"they are stronger than we,"* 13:31), the Israelites were not just being modest. They were persistently, knowingly disobeying the clear voice of God and repeated instructions given to them from on high. Theirs was not a momentary loss of nerve or lapse of faith; it was a "set in their ways," Garden of Eden choice to follow the voice of the serpent rather than the divine voice. The complaining was nothing short of "wickedness," "despising," and "rebellion" (vv. 9ff).

God wants to take them out (v. 12), but Moses talks God off the ledge from doing so (vv. 13ff). Still, short of wiping them out, God issues consequences for those who "have tested me ten times." None of them will see the Promised Land. More poignantly, their children will "suffer for your faithlessness" and wander around in the desert an extra forty years, "for every day (of persistent faithlessness) a year" (vv. 33f). Even after this proportionate verdict, the Israelites persist in presumption and disobedience, ignoring God's warnings about an attack (vv. 41ff).

What happens to people who insist on ignoring, distorting, and disobeying the will of God? Numbers 14 says that bring death on themselves and hell on their descendants.

C. S. Lewis famously said, "All that are in hell choose it." Hell is God giving people exactly what they want. Those who live in hell after they die have persistently chosen hell on earth, extending the arc of their lives into eternity. As Lewis puts it, "All God does in the end with people is give them what they most want."

What can a leader do in the face of wicked complainers? In the end, sadly, we can do little more than leave them to the consequences of their destructive choices. Pray for God's mercy on them. Don't be swayed by their terrible choices. Never believe that the majority is right just because it is the majority. Don't be fooled that "louder is profounder." Keep your eyes on the Promised Land and your ear tuned to the guiding voice of God.

Exercise: *Is there someone in your life whose complaining is clearly from insistent refusal to listen to God? If so, first, pray for this person's deliverance, just as Jesus taught us to pray for our enemies (Matthew 5:44). Then, resolve to listen to the voice of God rather than the voices of those who don't.*

"You have the fringe so that, when you see it, you will remember all the commandments of the Lord and do them, and not follow the lust of your own heart and your own eyes." – Numbers 15:39

Strangely inserted into the middle of stories of rebellion, Numbers 15 interrupts the story flow with a list of worship instructions. It breaks the narrative like a halftime speech to a team not following its game plan, urging the players back to fundamentals before the second half.

Praying New Beginnings

All of the back-to-basics instructions pertain to worship. There are specific matters of *"offerings"* (vv. 1-12, 17-21), equitable justice for the *"native"* and *"alien"* (vv. 13-16), *"atonement"* and reconciliation (vv. 22-31), and *"sabbath"* enforcement (vv. 32-36). Symbolizing obedience to these matters of worship, the Israelites are to wear *"fringes on the corners of their garments"* (v. 37) as a visual reminder. The clothing helps them to remember not to follow their own *"lust,"* as they have done in the rebellions of chapters 11-14. It is a visual reminder to worship carefully as a way to get back on track. The people had been spiraling into bad habits, and worship instructions are like a circuit-breaker. They attempt to interrupt, reboot, and restart. They refocus people on their core tasks as a way of course-correction, clarifying where they are heading and what it will take to get there.

Legendary UCLA basketball coach John Wooden famously began the first practice of the year with instructions on how to tie your shoes properly. Highly-touted recruits raised eyebrows, but the coach was establishing something important: if you never do the first things well, you won't do the later and bigger things well.

And just as Moses tried to break the circuit by reminding people how to worship, so a leader today must sometimes, in the face of trouble, return to "first things first."

Exercise: *Is there a troubling situation you are being called to engage? If so, what are some spiritual fundamentals you need to remember and reinforce as you do so? Name a few of these, and focus on doing them worshipfully and well as a start.*

Numbers 16

LIMINAL LEADERS

"He stood between the dead and living; and the plague was stopped." – Numbers 16:48

Numbers 16 captures multiple "revolt stories" of the people rising up against Moses and Aaron. It is something like a "greatest hits" summary of accusations they faced from those they were trying to serve. The common accusation against them is that *"you exalt yourselves above the assembly of the Lord"* (v. 3). Leaders can be expected to be different from the rest of the people and then criticized when they are! *"You have gone too far,"* they say. *"All of the*

Praying New Beginnings

congregation (and not just "you") *are holy, every one of them, and the Lord is among them"* (v. 3). They insinuate that Moses and Aaron put themselves above everyone else as "special."

But rather than exalting themselves *"above"* the people, or striking back at them, Moses and Aaron instead stand *"between"* the rebellious people and the Lord who is so angry that he will wipe out many of them with earthquake (v. 31), fire (v. 35), and plague (v. 46). Moses and Aaron lead by serving consistently ungrateful and misguided people, acting as a buffer between them and the lethal consequences of their envy.

Anthropologist Victor Turner described "liminality" as the state of a ritual leader standing on the threshold between old and new ways. In his essay, *"Betwixt and Between: The Liminal Period of Rites of Passage,"* the leader separates from the tribe, risking both ridicule from home and danger of the great unknown. Hierarchy disappears, and like a crab between molts, the leader is quite vulnerable.

Leaders are liminal in that they can be attacked by the very people they serve. Their very service of "riding the point" can be misinterpreted as ego. Get used to it. It's what leaders do and it comes with the territory. The trick is to maintain a servant heart toward complainers, and to let God take care of bringing them to account for misbehavior.

Exercise: *Is someone you are trying to serve "biting the hand that feeds them?" If so, how can you prevent their misbehavior from poisoning your heart toward them or toward service? Ask God to release you from any desire to respond to evil with evil. Ask for wisdom to lead "out in front" even though it may be misinterpreted.*

THE DESIGNATED LEADER

"And the staff of the man whom I choose shall sprout;
thus I will put a stop to the complaints of the Israelites
that they continually make against you."
– Numbers 17:5

Interpreters have had a field day with the symbolism of this episode. Some say Aaron's budding almond rod hearkens back to the Tree of Life in the Garden of Eden in Genesis 2, or the rod that Moses and Aaron threw down before Pharaoh in Exodus 7. Others say it foreshadows the messianic stump of Isaiah 11, the hyssop branch of John 19, and even the cross itself.

This speculation is all well and good, but the plain meaning of the chapter is valuable for its leadership insights. In the previous chapter, there has been an egalitarian uprising where jealous people resent the special status of Moses and Aaron as leaders. "One person, one vote," they seem to say. This is not new; in 12:2, the people complained, *"Has the Lord only spoken through Moses?"* Groups undergoing testing can revert to a democratic ideal that no one person should be "the" leader.

But Numbers 17 puts an end to that. God has called all the people, yes. But God, in choosing to cause Aaron's almond staff to blossom, has chosen him for a distinct, public, and priestly role. Moses kept the staff visible *"as a warning to rebels"* (v. 10) in hopes of scaring them out of complaining. It is a symbol of Aaron's unique calling – and that is not for trifling!

The designated leader must be humble, just as Moses was (12:3). But humility doesn't mean escaping the fact that the group's leader is <u>not</u> just like everyone else. When we have been called as the leader of a group, there is no escaping the reality that we are more visible, we bear unique responsibility, we will be held to a higher level of accountability, and we are a model for many rather than simply responsible for ourselves. Accepting this mantle is not just a hard pill to swallow for those who want a total democracy. It is also a responsibility that the leader must accept and humbly live into.

Exercise: *Is there a situation in which you are "the designated leader" right now? If so, what are a couple of your unique responsibilities? Pray for the grace to accept these, the humility not to take advantage of your power, and the courage to carry them out as an example for others.*

Numbers 18

NOT BEHOLDEN

"You shall incur no guilt by reason of it, when you have offered the best of it. But you shall not profane the holy gifts of the Israelites, on pain of death."
– Numbers 18:32

Designated spiritual leaders (Aaron's sons and the Levites) have been set apart *"as a gift"* (v. 6) to the whole people, and they bear unique *"responsibility"* and *"duties"* (vv. 1-3) as leaders. Interestingly, this chapter focuses not on those specific roles as much as it does the spiritual leader's relationship with money. Two highlights stand out:

1. It is good and right that the spiritual leader be paid out of the offerings of the people, rather than having the normal income of *"allotment in their land"* (v. 20). Paul would later remind the church of this in I Corinthians 9.

2. The spiritual leader, reciprocally, was both to serve *"as a gift"* to the people, and also to *"set apart an offering from it to the Lord, a tithe of the tithe"* (v. 26).

Thus on one hand, the spiritual leader is not beholden to the people based on their financial support. God sets the non-optional percentage for people to give, and the leader can't be "bought." On the other hand, the leader is to model and demonstrate faithful generosity for the rest of the people in giving *"a tithe of the tithe"* (one-tenth of received gifts) back to God from what was received. Failing to do so was to *"profane"* gifts and to summon *"pain of death!"*

Here, the spiritual leader's finances are on public display. Leaders can't be manipulated based on how much or how little the people give. Leaders also model giving for others. When both things happen, the spiritual leader is not beholden, not owned, free to serve people and be faithful to God.

Exercise: *Take a fearless, searching personal financial inventory: is there any area of your financial life that, if on public display, would "profane," pollute, or compromise your ability to lead well? Are you able to receive gratefully gifts from others without being distorted in how you lead them? Are you being as generous as you should be?*

Numbers 19

INTERPETING DEATH

"Those who touch the dead body of any human being shall be unclean. They shall purify themselves with the water on the third day and on the seventh day, and so be clean ...." – Numbers 19:11-12

After the previous chapters make a big deal out of the special importance of a set-apart spiritual leader, Numbers 19 turns to the work of that priestly leader. Much of what is described in the chapter is time-bound and tribe-specific; we no longer need to worry today with *"hyssop,"* sprinkling *"blood,"* and burning *"heifers"* (vv. 2ff).

But when you take a bigger-picture look at the work of spiritual leaders, what you see here is that much of their work is to help those in their community deal well with death. This could be the death of something sacrificed (the previously mentioned *heifer*), or, more importantly, what to do in the community when there is a *"corpse"* (vv. 11ff). What does a community do when someone in it dies? How is that handled well (or poorly)? What are the proper ceremonies? How are those touched by death brought through the experience and back to a state of restoration? How does one move from death to a state of *"cleansing"* (v. 20)?

These are big questions and that is delicate work. The spiritual leader does this work because, while difficult, it is so necessary. Handling death poorly leads to all kinds of problems – what the chapter calls *"uncleanness, impurity,* and *defilement."* But entering these painful situations, fully acknowledging their significance, and helping others move through them – that is a great work of leadership.

One of the great ways we are able to serve people around us is to help them deal with the death around them. Every day, people are, in small ways and large, cut off from community because of their grief and inability to move through death. When we enter those realms of loss and pain, help them interpret death, and move others toward restoration in the community, we have done a great work of spiritual leadership.

Exercise: *Pray for someone you know who is being shaken badly by death (either recent or longstanding). Ask God to reveal to you how you can enter their realm of loss and serve that person.*

Numbers 20

LEGITIMATE REQUEST

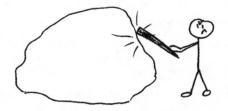

ILLEGITIMATE RESPONSE

"Then Moses lifted up his hand and struck the rock twice with his staff; water came out abundantly, and the congregation and their livestock drank. But the Lord said to Moses and Aaron, "Because you did not trust in me, to show my holiness before the eyes of the Israelites, therefore you shall not bring this assembly into the land that I have given them." – Numbers 20:11-12

This is a story of legitimate requests met with illegitimate responses, leading to everyone looking bad. The people are thirsty, and a request for water is a legitimate need. But they come off as rebellious, ungrateful, and whiny. Miriam and Aaron, clearly important community leaders, pass away almost unnoticed (v. 1) or even perhaps shamed (vv. 26-28).

And Moses, while meeting the needs of the people for water, does so by lashing out with his words and striking the rock twice. The story says that his action is angry, quarrelsome, unholy, and untrusting. It ensures he will not enter the Promised Land (vv.10-13). Wow, is God giving the death penalty for jaywalking?! What is this story trying to teach us?

Perhaps the clue is the brief episode of Edom not permitting Israel to pass through its territory (vv. 18-21). Because of old and unhealed wounds, unstated but real grievances, Israel has to go the long way on its journey. Could this be a metaphor for what happens when we are "junked up" relationally? Reasonable requests go unmet because of simmering unseen infections?

While much of the story puzzles, this much is clear: our "issues" always "leak." If there is an undercurrent of anger, pride, hurt, or rebellion in our hearts, it will surely manifest itself in our decisions. We may make the right calls, but will do so with a bitterness or pride that poisons outcomes. Good leaders attend to any funk in their soul so that it doesn't corrupt even their technically correct decisions.

Exercise: *Is there any long-standing poison of bitterness, entitlement, or indignation in your heart? Can you identify its source? Begin to ask God to drain the swamp of those underground feelings. In the meantime, ask for grace not to have your anger "leak out" onto your daily interactions and decisions.*

John P. Chandler

HEALING
THE
MISERABLE

*"So Moses made a serpent and put it on a pole; and whenever a serpent bit someone, that person would look at the serpent of bronze and live." – **Numbers 21:9***

Moses' grace to the people he led was not to ditch them when they were at their worst. Taking the long and hard path through the hot wilderness, the people simultaneously complain that *"there is no food"* and *"we detest this miserable food"* (v. 5). This was more than whining; it was outright rejection of God and rebellion against Moses.

God sends judgment against the people in the form of fiery serpents. Moses the leader responds to the crisis well. He:

- Remains in their midst during hard times; *"the people came to Moses"* (v. 7);

- Hears their confession: *"We have sinned against the Lord and against you";*

- Prays for the people rather than responding with bitterness or revenge (v. 8);

- Responds to God's direction to create a *"serpent of bronze … upon a pole"* by which people could be healed.

The Greeks later appropriated this symbol of a serpent on a pole as the rod of Asclepius, symbol for medical healing. The gospel of John says that it foreshadows another who was lifted upon a pole, the work of Jesus Christ on the cross, for the healing of the world (John 3:14).

With a leadership lens, what we see here in the work of Moses (and later Jesus) is the perseverance to remain immersed in the suffering of the miserable until they can find a way out. It is easy to withdraw from the miserable. But as good nurses and doctors today still practice, leaders in the spirit of Moses hang in there with them and so are part of a path to healing.

Exercise: *Is there a miserable person from whom you would prefer to withdraw, but toward whom God is asking you to move? Practice the discipline of not leaving until you build the muscle for doing this well.*

Numbers 22

SERIOUS PURPOSE. LIGHT MANNER

"Then the Lord opened the mouth of the donkey, and it said to Balaam, "What have I done to you that you've struck me these three times?" Balaam said to the donkey, "Because you have made a fool of me!"
– Numbers 22:28-29

There are all kinds of serious messages conveyed in the saga of Balaam and Balak. For instance:

- Prophets should not be "bought" – *"Although Balak were to give me his house full of silver and gold, I could not go beyond the command of the Lord my God, to do less or more"* (v. 18).

Praying New Beginnings

- The people of God sometimes venture into alien territory but are to remain faithful even there – "... *get up and go with them; but do only what I tell you to do"* (v. 20).

- The purposes of God are irresistible, more powerful than human kings – *"for I know that whomever you* (God) *bless is blessed, and whomever you curse is cursed"* (v. 6).

However, we remember Balaam primarily for the hilarious story of his conversation with a donkey. In the heart of profound stories about rebellion is this humorous folk tale about overcoming stubbornness and foolishness to set a prophet on the right path. We have to ask why the book of Numbers would put such a satire in the heart of a narrative of rebellion.

The answer, of course, is that sometimes humor and parable are the best ways to get past defensive listeners and get the point across. Sometimes the shortest distance between two points is not a straight line of direct command, but a funny parabola that moves indirectly from point "A" to point "B" through a lighter, more subtle touch. As preacher Fred Craddock taught, "Seriousness of purpose does not always require heaviness of manner." Sometimes important truths can be conveyed out of a funny story of a donkey being smarter than its rider.

Leaders are not flippant or silly. But sometimes they know how to get their point across without hammering people over the head with it.

Exercise: *Is there a serious and tricky situation you are facing that might be handled better with a lighter touch? How can you move forward responsibly (not being flip) but doing so with a wink and smile rather than a stern forehead?*

Numbers 23-24

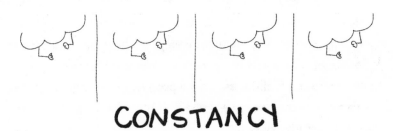

CONSTANCY

"But Balaam answered Balak, "Did I not tell you, "Whatever the Lord says, that is what I must do?" So Balak said to Balaam, "Come now, I will take you to another place; perhaps it will please God that you may curse them for me from there." – Numbers 23:26-27

Here are three scenes between Moabite king Balak and prophet of the Lord, Balaam. Balaam, who had been as stubborn as a mule, was (ironically) broken of his stubbornness by a talking donkey in chapter 22. Now he has to break the stubbornness of a Moabite king who wants to hire the prophet to curse his enemies. Offering to pay handsomely, Balak wants to bribe the prophet to say what the king wants said. He's trying to "hire" a divine curse.

Praying New Beginnings

But the prophet won't budge, and so it takes three scenes and four oracles for the argument to run its course. One of the king's strategies is to move the prophet to *"another place,"* a different location. He believes that if he can just get the prophet to see things from another perspective, he can persuade him to change his mind. The king tries bribery, tries persistence, and tries shifting the venue. But the prophet only speaks the word God gives him. Why? Because, he says, *"God is not a human being, that he should lie, or a mortal, that he should change his mind"* (23:19).

Because God has this unchanging constancy of character, the prophet cannot be inconsistent in reporting the words of God. Neither desire for reward, threat of punishment, persistent badgering, nor shifting locations can change any of that.

When leaders share what they believe is God-given vision, they understand that there will be opposition. The opposition can take many forms, sometimes carrot and sometimes stick. It sounds quite reasonable to be asked to reconsider from another point of view. But if the character of God is constancy and the message from God is clear, the leader has to match persistent temptation with equally unwavering faithfulness.

Exercise: *Ask God to reveal to you the difference in your heart between mulish stubbornness and faithful constancy that overcomes persistent temptation. Ask the Lord to make you tender enough to change course when he directs you to do so, and tough enough not to change course when others try to pull you off track.*

SOFT
REBELLIONS

=

HARD
CONSEQUENCES

"... the people began to have sexual relations with the women of Moab. These invited the people to the sacrifices of their gods, and the people at and bowed down to their gods. Thus Israel yoked itself to the Baal of Peor, and the Lord's anger was kindled against Israel."
– Numbers 25:1-3

When the first census was taken before the march through the wilderness (chapter 1), Israel had huge numbers, big vision, and terrified enemies. Even a donkey (chapter 22) and pagan king (chapters 22-23) could see that. By the second numbering in 26:51,

God has miraculously sustained the population, but the body count of dead first-generation rebels is staggering. Only Joshua and Caleb survived (26:65). How did a whole generation start strong but fail to finish?

It was not war with a powerful enemy from the outside, but the "soft" internal rebellions of apostasy, idolatry, and compromise that ruined them. The pioneers were done in by bad sex (v. 1) and intermarriage, by hanging around the wrong places (v. 2a), and by sitting down at the wrong tables to eat (v. 2b). Israel wasn't bearing witness in its consorting with foreigners but selling out the faith and mission in order to satisfy their own cravings. The consequences of their friendly but deadly compromises were almost unspeakably violent, including impaling (v. 4), public execution (v. 8), and a *"plague"* that killed *"twenty-four thousand"* (v. 9).

Paul would later chastise a fornicating church for bad sexual and eating practices by saying, *"Or do you not know that your body is a temple of the Holy Spirit within you?"* (1 Corinthians 6:19). Sexuality (the *body*) in inseparable from spirituality (the *temple*). We can be as at-risk spiritually though deadly dalliances as by hostile attack. Innumerable leaders have been done in despite great strengths through sexual sell-outs and giving away the heart of integrity that comes with such. This episode in Numbers is word to the wise to be on guard.

Exercise: *Is there anything going on with you sexually or relationally that could threaten your integrity as a follower of God and influencer of others? If so, confess your sin to God and one other trusted friend, stop what is inappropriate* <u>*immediately,*</u> *and ask for help to contain the plague and move in a better direction.*

John P. Chandler 271

Numbers 27

GOOD HANDOFFS

"Not one of them was left, except Caleb son of Jephunneh and Joshua son of Nun. Then the daughters of Zelophehad came forward." **– Numbers 26:65-27:1**

"You shall give him (Joshua) some of your authority, so that all the congregation of the Israelites may obey." **– Numbers 27:20**

Numbers 27 begins and ends with succession stories. Since the whole first generation that began in the wilderness died off (except Joshua and Caleb), the second generation had to take the mantle. Since the sons who would normally inherit the job were gone, *"the daughters came forward."* Since Moses was not the one to lead them to cross into the Promised Land (vv. 12ff), he had to appoint Joshua as a successor.

Praying New Beginnings

Each succession story illustrates a positive and negative aspect of spiritual leadership. Negatively, there had to be successors because the predecessors either sinned, failed, or weren't around to finish. Moses *"rebelled"* and the people *"quarreled"* with God so decisively and persistently that it was clear that they were not spiritually fit to see the task through. The first generation of men likewise died off because of sin, leaving the women to inherit the responsibility – a remarkable statement in a patriarchal age. Sometimes the road from yesterday to today is not the same as the road from today to tomorrow.

Positively, though, these handoffs went well. Moses ruled wisely to entrust both the daughters of Zelophehad and also Joshua with leadership. He was a good predecessor in ensuring the success of his successors.

Good leaders accept when it is time for the next generation of leaders to step forward. Thus, as Moses did, they make rulings, consult God, and work with the people to create the conditions for the people to thrive with someone else at the helm. Scores of good leaders who have run well either refuse to give up the ball when it is time, or they botch the handoff. But Moses was one who set up Joshua to succeed him ... and to succeed in leading the people.

Exercise: *How will you know when it is time to pass the mantle, and to whom to pass it, in an area where you are currently the decision-maker? Envision what a good handoff will look like. Ask God how to invest now in a successor and to begin creating the conditions in which s/he can thrive.*

John P. Chandler   273

Numbers 28-29

OCCUPATIONS AND OFFERINGS

"You shall not work at your occupations."
– Numbers 28:18, 25f, 29:1, 12, 35

As the next-generation leaders come in, Moses passes along the commands of God to them. On the surface, these two chapters contain commands about offerings for various occasions. Below the surface they are about rhythm of life, and specifically about the rhythm of work and worship.

Praying New Beginnings

Seven times in the two chapters Moses warns the people, "*You shall not work at your occupations*" when giving these offerings. It seems that the great rival to giving appropriate thanksgiving to God and to acknowledging God as the center of life and the community is "*work.*" Imagine that!

Our work is a gift from God. From Adam, we were "*put in the garden of Eden to till it and keep it,*" and to "*be fruitful and multiply and fill the earth*" (Genesis 2:15, 1:28). But work is fallen with sin, just like everything on the earth, and it craves a distorted, all-consuming role in our lives. A calendar of Sabbath, festivals, and offerings in which we are explicitly not permitted to work is the antidote. It resets our rhythm of life to that of creation, where God's six days of work are followed by a day of Sabbath rest and worship. It gives place for the values of rest and restoration, for celebration and gratitude, to grow in our lives.

There is no wisdom in working seven days a week. Doing so puts us out of rhythm with God and creation. And being fully occupied with work also makes it impossible for us to give the "*offerings*" to God that shapes our lives with thankfulness and forgiveness. Your occupation is important and God-given. Is it so important that it should consume your life to the point of displacing sanity, rhythm, gratitude, and reconciliation?

Exercise: *Mark one day of your calendar this week with a "No Occupations" notice. At the end of that day, take note of whether you were able to refrain from working. What were the temptations, if any? What was difficult about leaving your work behind for that period? What else had room to grow in the absence of work?*

John P. Chandler 275

"When a man makes a vow to the Lord, or swears an oath to bind himself by a pledge, he shall not break his word; he shall do according to all that proceeds out of his mouth."
– Numbers 30:2

As Moses passes on leadership to the next generation, his foundational instructions from the Lord are about "work-worship" rhythm (chapters 28-29) and, in this chapter, vow-keeping. The two are connected. Most vows were made in the context of offering sacrifices (29:39). Vows were requests for divine deliverance in dangerous situations. People would often abstain from needs (like food) to indicate the vow's seriousness.

While Numbers 30 clearly represents an unsavory patriarchy, its idea that vows are communal is worth keeping. Parents are responsible for the tacit approval of children's vows, as are spouses and other members of the tribe. We have to help each other keep our promises. Vow-keeping is indispensible to the vitality and integrity of the community. We hold our closest relationships accountable for their vows to God; if we don't, then we *"bear guilt"* (v. 15) together!

When people make vows, it is not only a vertical transaction between that person and the Lord. It also affects the community horizontally. A community centered in the worship of the God of the Bible helps one another keep promises.

Exercise: *Review any vows (substantial life-altering promises) that you have made. Who are the people helping you to keep those vows? Don't be afraid to ask for their help today!*

John P. Chandler 277

PAYOFF FOR ROOTING OUT CORRUPTION

"Everything that can withstand fire, shall be passed through fire, and it shall be clean. Nevertheless it shall also be purified with the water for purification; and whatever cannot withstand fire, shall be passed through the water." – Numbers 31:23

There is no getting around the violence and vengeance of Numbers 31. Moses' instructs next-generation leaders to execute holy war: *"avenge the Israelites on the Midianites"* (v. 1). Their ancient rival had not only been an enemy in war, but a source of internal corruption *"so that the plague came among the congregation of the Lord"* (v. 16).

However, this is really a story about the effects of *"purification,"* about *"fire"* and *"water."* The mind-numbing details of the spoils of war unlock the core meaning of the chapter. An army of 12,000 Israelites not only destroys the rival army, but brings home booty of over 800,000 animals, 32,000 virgins, and nearly fifty pounds of gold – all without a single Israelite casualty (v. 49). These fantastic amounts clue us to understand that the description of the holy war is theology. The second generation who is diligent to root out corruption experiences fantastic fruitfulness. This war is a dress rehearsal for the people of God who will soon occupy a pagan Canaan. They will forever have to deal with purifying corruption.

So skip the ancient bloodshed and focus on this contemporary takeaway: when leaders root out widespread corruption, there is a huge payoff. It is unsavory work, and your hands will be dirty with war, requiring the cleansing work that purifies with *"fire"* and *"water."* But the payoff of taking back corrupted territory is *"tribute for the Lord"* (v. 28), *"a memorial"* (v. 54) for the fighters, and *"atonement"* (v. 50) for the people.

Prayer: *"God of Israel, make me think at least twice before declaring holy war against anyone or anything. But neither let me be complacent in the face of corruption which damages your world. I ask for the humility never to be self-righteous, but the courage not to back down from leading the battle against wrong-doing. Help me, in this, to follow in the way of Jesus, who both accepted the cross and cleansed the temple. It is thus in Jesus' name that I pray, Amen."*

John P. Chandler   279

Numbers 32

VANGUARDS

"We will build sheepfolds here for our flocks and towns for our little ones, but we will take up arms as a vanguard before the Israelites, until we have brought them to their place." – Numbers 32:16-17

As Israel prepares for the war necessary to cross into the Promised Land, two of its twelve tribes balk. The *"Reubenites"* and *"Gadites owned a very great number of cattle"* and preferred to end the journey and settle for grazing than to fight and cross the Jordan (vv. 1-5). They don't want to put their families and flocks at risk.

Praying New Beginnings

Moses views this as flat-out rebellion, calling them *"a brood of sinners"* and likening the reluctance to a previous generation's abandonment of their calling (vv. 6-15). Chastened, these two tribes decide to join the fight alongside the rest of the Israelites. After doing their part in war, they will be given the blessing to return to settle in their *"sheepfolds"* and *"towns."*

Specifically, these two tribes will take up arms as a *"vanguard before the Israelites"* in war. *"Vanguard"* is a very unusual word, found only here and Deuteronomy 3:18 in the NRSV. The Hebrew connotes "hurrying." Like scouts Joshua and Caleb of a previous generation, these tribes will *"take up arms to go before the Lord for the war"* (v. 20), assuming the risk of going out ahead of the army on the front lines of the fight. (This mission was accomplished in Joshua 22.)

The image of a *"vanguard"* is a powerful one for leadership. A leader "hurries" ahead of the rest of the people, assuming front-edge and perhaps disproportionate risk. That leader may be reluctant or self-interested on some levels. Nonetheless, they overcome their fears, make their promises, and hurry out in front of the tribe. They do their part by moving out beyond their own interests, serving by leading.

Exercise: *Do a self-inventory about your motives and fears related to moving forward into a risky venue (rather than staying behind comfortably where you are.) Ask the Lord to deal with any sin in you, and ask God to help you be a vanguard when you are called to hurry to the front ahead of others.*

Numbers 33

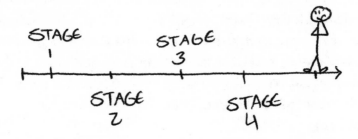

LEARNING FROM THE STAGES

"But if you do not drive out the inhabitants of the land from before you, and those whom you let remain shall be as barbs in your eyes and thorns in your sides; they shall trouble you in the land where you are settling. And I will do to you as I thought to do to them."
– Numbers 33:55-56

Praying New Beginnings

"These are the stages by which the Israelites went out ... under the leadership of Moses and Aaron," begins Numbers 33. The chapter is records the journey "stage by stage" (v. 2), recounting the critical chapters of the journey from Egypt to the edge of the Promised Land. Why is there a point-by-point recitation of the race at the edge of the finish line?

The answer lies in the closing warnings to the Israelites. Unless they "drive out the inhabitants of the land" into which they are entering, "they shall trouble you in the land where you are settling." Using very unusual vocabulary, Numbers warns Israel that doing the job half-way will lead to "barbs in your eyes and thorns in your sides." Anything short of total obedience will have grave consequences. Israel must sprint through the finish line.

So the point of recounting the history is as an object lesson. The people of God are to learn from the "stages" of their journey. There is a body of knowledge they acquire by studying the trajectory of their walk with God. And if they fail to learn from their history, their future will be full of "barbs" and "thorns."

A good leader helps set context for others. They help people see mileposts and plot out spiritual markers of their journey, which sketches out a bigger picture of the map of what God has done and may be doing next in their lives. A leader helps others learn from the stages.

Exercise: *Plot five or six stages which recount your life on a piece of paper using words, phrases or short sentences. Is there anything about this graph which gives you a clue to what God might want to do next in and through your life?*

John P. Chandler   283

Numbers 34-35

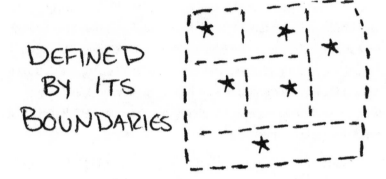

DEFINED
BY ITS
BOUNDARIES

*"This is the land that shall fall to you for an inheritance,
the land of Canaan, defined by its boundaries."*
– Numbers 34:2

Full of bright hope, Numbers 34-35 anticipates Israel's occupying *"Canaan,"* the Promised Land lying at the end of their journey through the desert. On the threshold of entering, *"The Lord spoke to Moses, saying: Command the Israelites …"* (34:1). What would God's just-before-the-big-moment instruction be? It is two chapters about the *"boundaries of the land."*

Praying New Beginnings

The tribal leaders are told, lot by lot, whom is to live where. The first time these leaders were listed (chapter 1) is the inauguration of the march. The second listing (chapter 13) marks the decisive rebellion of the faithless first generation. Would this third listing find faithful listening? It depends on whether the leaders and people heed the *"boundaries."*

These boundary markers are what delineate special *"towns that you give to the Levites"* and *"six cities of refuge"* where a *"slayer"* can await a fair trial instead of being avenged impulsively (35:6). In the Promised Land, there is to be a better way than angry retribution. There will be justice, fairness, grace, and places where decisions are made in holy reflection rather than through emotional outbursts. These are *"cities of refuge"* – and are marked by their *"boundaries."* Such places make it possible *"for I the Lord (to) dwell among the Israelites"* (35:34).

Every parent understands that toddlers want and need to know the rules. The new nation, Israel, certainly needed to grasp the idea of clear tribal property lines to get along (with each other and with those who were already in the land). A boundary is not an arbitrary imposition from the more powerful onto the weak. It is a loving gift that makes order, justice, and holiness possible in communal living. The people of God are always instructed, *"You shall not pollute the land in which you live"* (35:33). A good leader knows that setting clear boundaries is a big step toward a better community.

Exercise: *What is one clear boundary you need to keep for yourself? What is one boundary you need to set for others? Reflect on how these boundaries will promote "refuge" for your relationships.*

RETAINING
THE
INHERITANCE

"No inheritance shall be transferred from one tribe to another; for each of the tribes of the Israelites shall retain its own inheritance." – **Numbers 36:9**

Close families have been torn apart throughout human history over arguments about the inheritance. Numbers 36 is a case study about marriage, property transfer, and inheritance. It is a preemptive strike against any rupture in community over inheritance disputes. Here is a picture of how to deal well with the inheritance.

As such, it is a capstone expression of a second generation of sojourners who demonstrated that *"I the Lord dwell among the Israelites"* (35:34). Where the first generation bungled their Exodus inheritance and infuriated God, the second generation experienced God's dwelling among them. Compare:

First Generation (Numbers 1-26)	Second Generation (Numbers 27-36)
• Mechanical obedience (ch.1-10)	Respectful of authority but bold to ask for a reasonable compromise (vv. 5-9)
• Spiral of revolt in ch. 11-25	Faithful to tradition but negotiating for a new day
• Resisted legitimate spiritual authority and self-serving jockeying for power	Allows outgoing Moses to command, and humbly submits to "heads of ancestral houses" (v. 1), previous leaders
• Fear of enemies over fear of God	Bold faith to march into Canaan

A new generation does well to learn from the mistakes of a previous generation. In doing so, we can retain the best inheritance, prevent community rupture, finish the journey well, and be prepared to enter the Promised Land.

Exercise: *What is the truest inheritance you wish to receive from those who went before you? What do you need to leave behind from that previous generation in order faithfully to retain that inheritance and move forward into the next stage of the journey?*

John P. Chandler

Deuteronomy 1

*"Beyond the Jordan in the land of Moab, Moses
undertook to expound this law as follows: ...."*
– Deuteronomy 1:5

On the threshold of entering the Promised Land (Numbers
36:13), the book of Deuteronomy is a giant pause button in which
Moses warns the people of Israel before they enter. In three sermons
(chapters 1-4, 5-28, and 29-30), Moses reinterprets the Law (Exodus
20) given to a previous generation for a new day. Deuteronomy
means "second law," but it is a second law only in the sense that it is
a reapplication of the original Law to a new generation.

Praying New Beginnings

Moses' sermons are called "*expound(ing) the law.*" In 621 B.C., King Josiah would rediscover this book of sermons and issue sweeping reforms (2 Kings 22-23). And Jesus would likewise later say six times, in the Sermon on the Mount, "*You have heard that it was said ... but I say to you*" (Matthew 5:21-48). Moses, Josiah, and Jesus each do the leadership work of "expounding."

Every leader does this work of taking something that has existed and has been known for a long time, reinterpreting and reapplying it for a new day. Leaders don't typically have to reinvent but to rediscover, restore, and refresh things of value that have fallen into disuse or misuse. To speak as a leader is not to say something so original that no one has ever said before. It is rather to say old things in new ways, eliciting nods of recognition and "Aha!" moments from hearers. When we do this well, people remember again the forgotten ways, reaffirm old loyalties, and rediscover direction that may have gone off course.

Leaders, we don't need originals as much as we need better expounding!

Exercise: *What old truth do you need to dust off and reapply to your life and decision-making today? What is something you learned long ago that you have more or less forgotten and need to bring to the forefront of your interactions this week? Once you identify this wisdom, apply it several times to your thinking and speaking. Then, reflect on the impact of this "expounding."*

John P. Chandler   289

PICKING YOUR BATTLES

"... so be very careful not to engage in battle with them ...."

"Do not harass Moab or engage them in battle ..."

*"When you approach the frontier of the Ammonites, do
not harass them or engage them in battle ..."*
– Deuteronomy 2:4-5, 9, 19

The previous chapter (1:43) ends with a description of what happened when the people of God got in fights that God never wanted for them. They were *"chased as bees"* (1:44), and their weeping return was met with stony silence from God (1:45). Deuteronomy 2 climaxes with a (rare for the Bible) holy war of victory and destruction over *"Sihon"* (2:26-37) and *"Bashan"* (3:1-11). But before these fights, the key feature of the chapter are repeated warnings *"not to engage in battle"* with various enemies.

Once, Israel was *"not to engage in battle"* because the enemy was fearful (v. 4). Other times, it was to refrain because the Lord *"will not give you any of its land as a possession"* (vv. 9, 19). Only when there is direct instruction to fight is it said that God *"gave"* or *"handed over"* the enemy to Israel (2:33, 3:2). The only permitted wars were "holy wars." In other words, don't fight unless God has given you the direct command to fight – and has gone before you to fight for you (3:22).

There is a time and a season for everything under the sun, including a time to fight (Ecclesiastes 3:3, 8). But the rule of thumb in Deuteronomy is that the people of God are <u>not</u> to fight or *"engage in battle"* unless there is a specific command from God to do so. Good leaders stay out of wars unless they are holy wars.

Exercise: *Is your first reaction "fight" or "flight?" Of the serious conflicts you are engaged in (or are about to be engaged in), what do you need to learn from the example of this chapter about whether to engage in battle?*

Deuteronomy 3

"The Lord said to me, "Enough from you! Never speak to me of this matter again." – Deuteronomy 3:26

Moses is quite the hero in Deuteronomy. Throughout the book, he's the preacher giving his last sermons. In chapter 3, he's the lead worshiper, praising God and interceding for and serving the people (vv. 23f). When it is all said and done, Moses can be said to be the atoning figure who takes on the sin of his people so that they are free to cross over into the Promised Land (v. 26a).

Praying New Beginnings

But in this highly-charged incident, Moses pushes God to the brink and gets and angry slap-back. He asks God to revisit the incident of striking the rock at Meribah (Numbers 20) and reconsider the punishment that would prevent him from *"cross(ing) over to see the good land beyond the Jordan"* (v. 25). God interrupts the love-fest and rebukes Moses sharply, telling him never to bring up the subject again. The case is closed, never to be reopened. Once Moses accepts this, he is then able to *"charge Joshua, and encourage and strengthen him"* (v. 28) as the protégé who will succeed him in leadership.

There is a time to persist and keep chopping away at a difficult matter not easily resolved. But in some matters, a leader has to learn when the deal is done, the matter is settled, and the score is final. In those things, to continue to revisit, wish, and hope for a different outcome is a waste of time and sucks the energy from the "next" matters of your life and charge. A wise leader discerns when it is a matter of *"Enough!"* and spends energy on things that can be changed in the future.

Exercise: *Meditate on this portion of Reinhold Niebuhr's "Serenity Prayer":*

"God, give me the courage to change the things that I can change, The serenity to accept the things I cannot change, And the wisdom to know the difference."

Ask God to fill you today with what you need first: courage, serenity, or wisdom.

John P. Chandler

GOD'S GREAT NEARNESS

"You must observe them diligently, for this will show your wisdom and discernment to the peoples, who, when they hear all these statutes, will say, "Sure this great nation is a wise and discerning people!" For what other great nation has a god so near to it as the Lord our God is whenever we call to him?" – Deuteronomy 4:6-7

The twin poles of this sermon are the Land and the Law. Because the Land is a gift from God to Israel, observing the Law is the people's great response. Indeed, the Law itself is a gift, in that it makes possible the gracious ongoing relationship between the people and God.

But the law of the land is for more than internal purposes. Practicing it also bears witness to outsiders who watch its keepers. When those who do not know the Lord watch people who *"observe diligently,"* they experience *"wisdom and discernment."* They also see a God who is gloriously *"near"* to his people *"whenever we call to him."* Could this be available for us as well?

God's greatness is in his nearness, the availability to the beloved people who are in a vibrant relationship with him. Such transcendence close at hand is the witness of a people who *"diligently"* practice the habits of the Law of the Land.

A leader can lay down all kinds of rules for followers. But unless they are part of a winsome, vibrant, magnetic community easily witnessed and craved by outsiders, what is the point?

Exercise: *What is one spiritual habit that I keep that can be an inspiration to someone around me? How can I share about this practice in a way that does not sound self-righteous, but points to the nearness of God that I experience through it, and the possibility that others may experience the same availability of God?*

CHOOSING NOT TO DIE

"Today we have seen that God may speak to someone and the person may still live. So now why should we die?"
– Deuteronomy 5:24-25

Forty years after Sinai, on the banks of the Jordan, Moses here invites a new generation to become God's covenant people in their own time and place. The commandments are not simply ancient history to be recited. They beg to be reinterpreted for a new generation: *"Not with our ancestors did the Lord make this covenant, but with us, who are all of us here alive today"* (v. 3).

So how does a new generation live, in Walter Brueggemann's words, into this "alternative community of neighborliness?" The commandments are more than a set of rules. They sketch a vision of a different existence, of what is possible when people are transformed by drawing intentionally and "faithfully close to the power and purposes of God." This new generation remembers Exodus from slavery and Sinai, and begins to envision its own path to a new life and freedom and cause in the Promised Land.

Ultimately, everyone dies, and we don't get a vote in that. But we all get a vote while living as to whether to live a transformed and alternative existence. The gift of the commandments was the possibility of choosing a difficult and different but rewarding path. It opened the possibility of transformation. Keeping the commandments is always difficult. But not as difficult as dying!

Leaders set out clear, demanding visions of alternative existence. Their job is not to make it easy on people, but, using memory and hope, to make the hard and good life attainable and clear.

Exercise: *What is your difficult but attainable vision for the good life and good community? Can you name it clearly?*

Deuteronomy 6

"And when you eaten your fill, take care that you do not forget the Lord, who brought you out of the land of Egypt, out of the house of slavery. The Lord your God you shall fear; him you shall serve, and by his name alone you shall swear." – Deuteronomy 6:11-13

This is the great "Shema" (Hebrew for "Hear!") statement for Israel, the core message that they are to remember and pass along to their children. It is about the one God, one faith, and one call that they are commanded *"diligently"* to observe *"for our lasting good"* (vv. 24f).

The great threat to remembering, doing, and passing along is the level of abundance and blessing Israel will experience in keeping the commandments. Deuteronomy states it pretty starkly: if you *"observe them diligently ... it will go well with you in the land"* and you will

Praying New Beginnings

experience *"a land flowing with milk and honey"* (v. 3). If not – then not so much. So, the people of God are most at risk when they are full of the gifts God has given: *"fine, large cities that you did not build, houses filled with all sorts of goods that you did not fill ... olive groves that you did not plant"* (v. 11). When they are "full," they might *"forget the Lord."* Prosperity is a blessing, and also puts one at great risk.

The great antidote to the forgetting due to a full stomach is a triangle of *"fear, serve,* and *swear."* What is at stake are our attitudes, the promises we make, and to whom we are loyal:

Leaders remember that the rich and blessed have unique challenges and temptations. We can help those who have the most (including ourselves!) not to get swallowed by their gifts by challenging them to *"fear, swear,* and *serve"* the Giver of those gifts.

Exercise: *As you count your blessings, what first step might you take to remember God as the great Giver, diligently holding to your identity as one who hears and follows the Lord? What needs your first focus today: your attitude, your speech, or your behavior? How might you challenge yourself and one other person today to hear, observe and remember the Lord in these ways?*

Deuteronomy 7

TEMPTATION TO COMPARISON

"It was not because you were more numerous than any other people that the Lord set his heart on you and chose you – for you were the fewest of all peoples. It was because the Lord loved you and kept the oath that he swore to your ancestors, that the Lord brought you out with a mighty hand, and redeemed you from the house of slavery, from the hand of Pharaoh king of Egypt." – Deuteronomy 7:7-8

Once the people of God occupy a land of other peoples, the comparisons and mental competition begins. Israel would be tempted to despair when smaller and less powerful than other nations, and to destroy them if bigger. The Lord, on the other hand, warns them to avoid the temptation to compare at all.

Praying New Beginnings

God tells Israel that he did not choose the high bidder. God's love is based not in a beauty contest, but in the divine character. Such a covenant emanates both from a *"heart"* of *"love,"* and also a non-feelings-based *"oath"* made long ago. Who the object of love was in comparison to others never enters the picture. Nor should our love and identity in response be based on who we are compared to those around us. In fact, when the people of God are tempted to see themselves in comparison to the other nations, the verbs used to rebuke that are verbs of holy war: *"utterly destroy ... show no mercy ... break ... smash ... hew down ... burn"* (vv. 2-5). Love can never thrive in an environment of comparison.

Any love that reflects the divine character overcomes our cultural and human disposition to base love in a contest. Any decent leader ensures the loyalty of her or his people by basing their common life and mission on something greater than the next younger, sexier, or hipper thing passing by. Unless and until we can overcome the temptation to base our identity on comparison, we will struggle to lead in an environment of insecurity and pride, never out of confidence and clarity.

Prayer: *O Lord, thank you for loving me based not on who I am, but based on who you are. Help me today to love the people around me not because they compare favorably to others, but because they are persons of intrinsic worth and value. Out of this unshakable and loyal covenant together, help us to move faithfully in a fickle and competitive world, in the name of Jesus, Amen.*

John P. Chandler

Deuteronomy 8

TEMPTATION TO MISS THE POINT

"Remember the long way that the Lord your God has led you these forty years in the wilderness, in order to humble you, testing you to know what was in your heart, whether or not you would keep his commandments." – Deuteronomy 8:2

On the threshold of a new chapter of life, Moses pauses and asks those whom he leads to consider the extremities of their journey. They are to remember when they were "*humble and hungry*" so as to recall how the Lord fed them, and not by "*bread alone*" (vv.2ff). They are also urged to pause and reflect on their successes, so as to recall and affirm that their wealth is a gift from God, and not a product of their own cleverness or industry (vv. 17f).

The point is that we learn best at the extremes of our experiences. Whether poverty or prosperity, hardship or great abundance, the more pronounced our situation, the more likely we are to focus on the extremities themselves and miss the larger point of those experiences. We need to be reminded in both positive and negative stresses that the Lord is at work to form something in us beyond the experiences themselves. To revel in wealth or despair in hardship are temptations to forego the ultimate in favor of the immediate.

Good leaders help those around her or him step back from the stresses of their immediate situation and ask the larger questions of what greater thing is being formed in them. What is God trying to do within you through this experience? Where is God taking you in this journey? Why is this current state an irreducible part of that formation? These are gift-questions a leader has for those who need to learn from their stresses.

Exercise: *Today, ask yourself or a person you influence to reflect on a larger question of formation. What is the larger point of a current positive or negative stress in your life? What is God trying to form in you through "discipline" (v. 5)?*

Deuteronomy 9

"Know, then, that the Lord your God is not giving you this good land to occupy because of your righteousness; for you are a stubborn people. Remember and do not forget how you have provoked the Lord your God to wrath in the wilderness; you have been rebellious against the Lord from the day you came out of the land of Egypt until you came to this place." **– Deuteronomy 9:6-7**

If history is told by the victors, then the great temptation of those who have experienced divine deliverance is to re-tell their story with rose-colored glasses. We tend to forget our own shortcomings (and the grace of God) when we are about to conquer.

Thus Moses warns Israel not to get too proud when it stands on the threshold of the Promised Land. Warning them against being puffed up with self-righteousness, he uses strong words to describe their track record of resistance to God. They have been thoroughly *"stubborn," "forgetful"* and *"rebellious."* In case they don't believe them, Moses spends most of the next two chapters recounting some of their most famous instances of acting *"corruptly"* (v. 12).

There is no undoing past shortcomings, but the present is certainly malleable. We can alter how we view our past and interpret our history, either acknowledging the grace of God, or inferring that, because we have won, we must have been pretty good all along the way. We get to choose our story of "then" and "now." And if we choose to rewrite the past in a way that washes away our shortcomings, and interpret the present as if we have "made it" all on our own, then watch out – trouble is coming. Pride goes before a fall.

My colleague and friend Kathryn McElveen puts it this way: we have lots of options for choosing our stories of "then," "now," and "next." And the stories we decide to tell about "then" and "now" determine our story of "next."

Exercise: *As you think about one of your great blessings today, look at two stories of how that blessing came to be a part of your life – one story as if by your own merit, another as an act of the grace of God. Consciously rehearse the story of grace, giving humble thanks to God in your heart. And at some point today, choose to tell that story of grace to at least one other person.*

John P. Chandler

Deuteronomy 10

"Circumcise, then, the foreskin of your heart, and do not be stubborn any longer." – Deuteronomy 10:16

Deuteronomy 10 begins with a sermon about *"tablets of stone"* and ends with an exhortation to *"circumcise the foreskin of your heart."* Moses recounts how he had smashed the stone tablets on which the Ten Commandments had been written because the covenant between the people and God had already been broken before he

Praying New Beginnings

could descend from the mountain. This necessitated a second set of stone tablets (vv. 1-5), and a lot of prayer from Moses for God not to blot out the rebellious people (vv. 10f).

Ironically, what the hard-as-a-rock commandments aimed to produce was a change in the most tender of places of people. God's commandments aim to produce a relationship with people characterized by a *"heart of love"* and symbolized in circumcision, the cutting of the most sensitive part of a human body and seat of human generativity. The hard Law points to a God who has a special soft spot *"for the orphan and widow, and who loves the stranger"* (vv. 18f) – and who wants us to have the same soft heart.

This paradox points to one of the great truths of life with the God of the Bible: that all of our discipline and obedience is not to make us as <u>hard</u> as the stone tablets on which the Law is given. Rather, the Commandments want to make our hearts as <u>soft</u> as God's heart toward the most vulnerable among us. The more exacting we are in keeping the Law, the more open our hearts are to become to the weak. And as we do so, the more we become like God.

Exercise: *Name one widow, one orphan, and one stranger whom you know. Pray hard for each of those people by name now. Ask God to soften your heart to bless them in some way.*

John P. Chandler

Deuteronomy 11

DEPENDING ON RAIN

"For the land that you are about to enter to occupy is not like the land of Egypt, from which you have come, where you sow your seed and irrigate by foot like a vegetable garden. But the land that you are crossing over to occupy is a land of hills and valleys, watered by rain from the sky ...."
– Deuteronomy 11:10-11

Deuteronomy 11 climaxes a sermon that began in chapter 8. The sermon has warned Israel against giving in to temptations to compare themselves to other nations, temptations to pride, self-sufficiency, self-righteousness, and temptations to miss the whole point of keeping the Law. In this wind-up, Deuteronomy tells the

Praying New Beginnings

people that their lives depend on loyalty and obedience. *"Today"* (v. 8, and a key word repeated frequently to show urgency) *"keep this entire commandment."* *"Diligently observe, hold fast"* (v. 22).

The arresting image is that as people stand at the decision fork of *"blessing and curse"* (v. 26), their very ability to eat and survive depends on their obedience. New Canaan is not like the old Nile valley, watered through human engineering *"like a vegetable garden."* Toto, you are not in Kansas anymore! No, the new land is *"watered by rain from the sky,"* and the people's loyalty to their relationship with God will be mirrored by the giving or withholding of rain from the heavens. As farmers depend on rain not of their making, so the people of God will have to depend faithfully on God in a new land.

It is a stark picture, offensive to contemporary sensibilities, that fruitfulness or drought could directly reflect divine blessing or curse. But the sermon is intentionally that blunt: your very survival depends on your relationship with God. It is a matter of life and death. And if death, you'll know it very quickly, because the rains won't come.

There are times when we are called to such blunt speech and stark alternatives. Not everything is a matter of life and death. But some things are, chief among them our covenant relationship with God. A leader does not shy away from speaking straightforwardly about such things.

Exercise: *Is there a blunt conversation about black/white alternatives you need to have with someone? If you sense that there is, first, be sure that it is a matter of life and death. Second, be certain that it truly is a fork in the road and not a gray area. And finally, pray now for God to give you the courage to have that hard conversation.*

John P. Chandler

Deuteronomy 12

"Take care that you do not offer your burnt offerings at any place you happen to see." – Deuteronomy 12:13

Deuteronomy 12-26, the heart of Moses' sermon, focuses on cleaning up and firming up the habits Israel will need to live well as a spiritual minority in Canaan. This chapter is organized around four speeches about centralizing and purifying worship (vv. 2-7, 8-12, 13-19, 20-28), correcting sloppy habits and refocusing the people on the first three of the Ten Commandments.

Praying New Beginnings

The speeches begin with powerful verbs insisting on banishing random devotion. Worship, finally, is about what suits God, not about what we want. So Moses tells Israel to cease building roadside altars every time the urge hits them. Indeed, the people are to "*demolish, dispossess, break down, smash, burn, hew down, and blot out*" (vv. 2f) every potential rival to the worship of God. Only after ridding themselves of idolatrous habits are the people then free to take up the ways of worshiping the God of Israel.

Dallas Willard often quipped, "First clear the lot and then build the house." In other words, you have to get rid of some things before you can take up other things. Just as Israel had to purge itself violently before settling in a new land, so the people of God at all times have to eliminate some old practices before taking up new ones. We practice spiritual disciplines of abstinence first in order to clear space to practice disciplines of engagement.

Construction projects often begin with demolition projects. A good leader will help people with their "stop doing" list before adding new "start doing" responsibilities.

Exercise: *What is one habit I need to demolish, beginning today? As I begin to stop doing this, imagine the space that will be created for being centered on a new and good thing.*

John P. Chandler

ENTICEMENT

*"If anyone secretly entices you – even if it is your brother,
your father's son or your mother's son, or your own son or
daughter, or the wife you embrace, or your most intimate
friend – saying, "Let us go worship other gods whom neither
you nor your ancestors have known ... you must not yield to
or heed any such persons." – Deuteronomy 13:6, 8*

Unconditional loyalty is the name if the game when you are a minority people looking to live with faithfulness to God when the majority is going in another direction. Temptation can come from a dreamer (v. 1) or "scoundrels" (v. 13). Yet the greatest temptations away from covenant loyalty come not externally, but from those closest to us. It is not the soldier that shoots at you but the spy in your midst who poses the greatest threat.

For this reason, Deuteronomy 13 lists the closest relations of family and friendship – sibling, child, spouse, best friend – and says that enticement from these relations can prove most tempting of all when it comes to eroding primary loyalty to God. We can be swayed from the call of God by political or financial interests, or by pressure from opponents. But enticement from those closest to us can be most seductive of all.

Wayne Oates would sometimes introduce his wife to people as the most dangerous person in his life. Their marriage was extremely close; why would he do this? "Because," he would say, "she is the chief rival in my life for the affection and attention that rightly belongs to God."

It is one thing to beware obvious enemies and quite another to be alert to subtle derailing in our life and intentions by those closest to us. Wise people watch for both and brook no rivals – even friendly rivals – to their primary relationship with God

---

Exercise: *Who are the three or four people closest to you right now? Though they may be gifts in your life, in what ways might they also be a source of temptation or distraction to your relationship with God? Pray for alertness and wisdom in these relationships, especially if they threaten your primary allegiance to God.*

John P. Chandler

"In the presence of the Lord your God, in the place that he will choose as a dwelling for his name, you shall eat the tithe of your grain, your wine, and your oil, as well as the firstlings of your herd and flock, so that you may learn to fear the Lord your God always." – Deuteronomy 14:23

"You are children of the Lord your God," says Moses (v. 1). He then sets out instructions about how to act into this identity of being *"treasured people"* (v.2). At the heart of what distinguishes the *"chosen"* people of God from pagan neighbors is their worshipful life. And what makes up their worshipful life, according to Deuteronomy 14, is how they mourn (vv. 1f), eat, and spend.

Special restrictions of vv. 3-21 are ritual more than dietary. Forbidden foods most likely were associated with foreign worship. And requirements of the *"tithe"* (vv. 22-29) mark the people of God by their planned generosity. Much can be said about keeping kosher and giving the tithe, but in the broadest brush strokes this much is clear: the children of God are to eat well and give well. Specifically, the Bible instructs us to be more careful about what we eat and more intentionally generous in how we give. We are to be tighter with the diet and looser with the purse. It will express devotion to God and bring joy (v. 26) to the practitioner!

Seemingly mundane matters of food and money are the stuff of everyday life. And leaders understand that how we handle ourselves in these daily matters are fundamental to what sets us apart as children of the Lord – or not. In our culture, people who might consume less and give more will definite garner attention as outside of the mainstream.

Exercise: *Pray over and plan how you will eat today, and over some intentional and ongoing practice of financial generosity. Ask God to solidify your identity as his child as you eat and give, reshaping how you consume and outpour.*

John P. Chandler   315

Deuteronomy 15

"Do not be hard-hearted or tight-fisted toward your needy neighbor. You should rather open your hand, willingly lending enough to meet the need, whatever it may be. Be careful that you do not entertain a mean thought ...."
– Deuteronomy 15:7-9

The Old Testament is thoroughgoing in its concrete instruction about liberal generosity. God's people are to *"tithe"* (given 10% of what they earn) and bring first-fruits (v. 14) or special gifts of what has been given to them by God. Every *"seventh year"* (vv. 1ff) of Jubilee cancels oppressive debts and reboots a new start for the needy. Many types of sacrifices are prescribed as a matter of worship. All of these commands about generosity spring from remembrance of what was given to us when we were needy (v. 15).

But beyond external practices, the Bible also addresses our inner disposition in matters of generosity. Deuteronomy 15 instructs the people of God to *"give liberally and be ungrudging"* (v. 10). Our attitude to give matters. Having a *"heart"* of love for the poor will lead us to see them with our *"eyes"* and respond with our *"hands"* in generosity.

Heart → Eyes → Hands

Jesus heightened such teaching in the Sermon on the Mount, saying that *"righteousness"* and being *"perfect"* was a matter of our inner dispositions as much as our external actions (Matthew 5). Becoming a generous person begins with our attitude toward what we have been given by God. It leads us to see the needy around us. And it causes us to open our fists and share. When there is transformation of heart, eye, and hand, we are moving toward the hope of a society of blessing and justice.

Exercise: *Is God prompting your <u>heart</u> to be more open and generous to the needy today than you have been? Or is God asking you to have <u>eyes</u> to see them all around you in a new way? Or is your first work simply to open your <u>hands</u> in giving more liberally?*

John P. Chandler 317

BRINGING YOUR DISH TO THE PICNIC

*"Three times a year ... (you) shall not appear before the
Lord empty-handed; all shall give as they are able, according
to the blessing of the Lord your God that he has given you."*
– Deuteronomy 16:16-17

Moses instructs the people of God to carry out festivals celebrating the goodness of God three times a year. The festival of *"unleavened bread"* (Passover, vv. 1-8) helps them remember their identity as people delivered out of slavery by God. The *"festival of weeks"* (vv. 9-12, Pentecost) reminds them that the harvest is a gift to them from a generous God. The *"festival of booths"* (vv. 13-15) is a third cause to *"rejoice"* and *"celebrate"* (v. 14) at the extravagance of God.

When people appear at these festivals, they are warned not to show up *"before the Lord empty-handed."* Everyone is, instead, to *"give as they are able, according to the blessing of the Lord your God that he has given you."* Generosity is proportionate, and what is called for is not equal giving but equal sacrifice and response. Not everyone brings the same dish to the picnic, but everyone is to bring a dish to the picnic!

Interestingly, these words on giving come between words on proper worship (16:1-15) and wise justice (16:18ff). The connection between love of God (worship) and love of neighbor (justice) is generosity. Just as the Sabbath is a weekly circuit-breaker that helps us remember that what we have is gift, and not just earned, so also festivals help us to celebrate what has been given to us, and to do so by pouring it out on God and on others.

Exercise: *When is the next scheduled "festival" on your calendar? How many of these do you have planned for this year? Meditate on how you can plan these festivals, and how you can mark them with specific acts of generosity toward God and others.*

John P. Chandler 319

Deuteronomy 17

JUSTICE, NOT CHARISMA

"Justice, and only justice, you shall pursue, so that you may live and occupy the land that the Lord your God is giving to you." – **Deuteronomy 16:20**

"A copy of this law ... shall remain with him and he shall read in it all the days of his life, so that he may learn to fear the Lord his God, diligently observing all the words of this law and these statutes, neither exalting himself above other members of the community nor turning aside from this commandment ... ." – **Deuteronomy 17:19-20**

This chapter establishes something like Israel's version of the Supreme Court. In the Promised Land, there must be a reasoned alternative to the revenge-based system of "honor" that is still alive in some cultures today. True justice or fairness is vital for a good life in the good land. What are the requirements for justice? Codes of judicial conduct require that there must be:

- Diligent inquiry of facts (v. 4);
- Sufficient, accurate testimony (vv. 6f);
- A right to appeal (vv. 8f);
- Deliberation and accountability among court members (vv. 10f);
- Access to wise folk in hard cases (v. 9); and
- Knowledge of the Law of God (v. 18)

All of this is contrasted by a warning against being seduced by a *"king over me, like all the nations that are around me"* (v. 14). Don't be swayed, says Moses, by a charismatic personality who makes big promises; he's always, in the end, in it *"for himself"* (v. 17). The history of Israel's kings bears this out – most were in it, finally, for personal elevation rather than the common good.

It's always easier to follow whatever a personable leader says rather than deal with the rigors and consistencies of a legal process. But it's fool's gold to do so. At our best, we hold Law to be more important than the personality of the leader. It's not the charisma of the leader that matters. Only when there is the rule of Law can justice and fairness reign sustainably.

Prayer: *Lord, let me never be wrongly swayed by an over-promising leader. And never let me use my influence on another based solely on force of personality. Help me to honor fair laws and due process today, and to always uphold these around those whom I lead. I want to be fair to all, and ask for your grace to do so with consistency and intention, in the name of Jesus, Amen.*

John P. Chandler

Deuteronomy 18

TRUE VS. FALSE PROPHETS

"You may say to yourself, "How can we recognize a word that the Lord has spoken?" If a prophet speaks in the name of the Lord but the thing does not take place or prove true, it is a word that the Lord has not spoken. The prophet has spoken it presumptuously; do not be frightened by it."
– Deuteronomy 18:21-22

The people of God want to understand the will of God. And the coming death of long-time leader Moses, who has been reliable to speak that word, heightens their anxiety about how they are going to know and do God's will. How can we discern what God is saying, and who can we trust to be a *"prophet"* who will reliably communicate what God wants from us?

First, chapter 18 begins with a discussion about the *"priests,"* who will be go-to sources of help *"to minister in the name of the Lord"* (vv. 1-8). To know God's will, start with a conversation there.

Praying New Beginnings

Second, *"you must learn not to imitate the abhorrent practices of those nations"* (v. 9). Deuteronomy lists many common superstitious or pagan ways of trying to predict the future or know the will of the gods in verses 10-14. These range from the creepy (seeking *"oracles from the dead,"* v. 11) to the downright abominable – the trial by fire whereby one's children's lives are put at risk. None of these practices – divination, soothsaying, augury, sorcery, casting spells, consulting spirits – are acceptable ways of finding God's will.

Finally, 18:15 promises that God will *"raise up a prophet"* worth heeding. Not everyone who speaks in the name of the Lord is a prophet. And the prophet who *"presumes to speak in my name a word that I have not commanded the prophet to speak – that prophet shall die"* (v. 20). But the acid test for true prophetic revelation of God's will is simple: if the prophet's prediction comes to pass, it is from God; if not, it is false and presumptuous.

Ultimately, God's will is not revealed by mechanistic means easily manipulated through magical technique. It will come through a trustworthy prophet – which is why the center of the biblical story is about the person of Jesus Christ.

Exercise: *As you seek God's will for what is next, walk through this checklist of key questions:*

1. *How am I tempted to try to "control" the future?*

2. *Am I dabbling in any way with superstition?*

3. *With whom do I turn for conversation when needing guidance about the future?*

4. *How will I discern wisely between true and false prophets?*

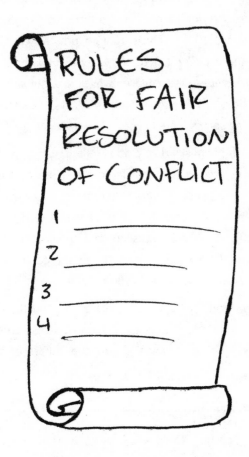

"Show no pity: life for life, eye for eye, tooth for tooth, hand for hand, foot for foot." – Deuteronomy 19:21

As the people of God move into a new land, there <u>will</u> be conflict. It is not a matter of "if" but "when!" Interestingly, Deuteronomy 19 deals with intra-community conflict rather than justice between Israel and other *"nations"* (v. 1). Family feuds are the hottest, and here is where the people of God need the most instruction. Accordingly, this chapter sets out at least four principles of how to resolve inevitable interpersonal friction:

1. _Provide "cities of refuge"_ (vv. 1-13). Rather than being ruled by the rage of revenge or by _"pity,"_ have places where everyone can cool off, collect evidence, and issue a ruling rationally rather than emotionally.

2. _Respect previously agreed-upon "boundaries"_ (v. 14). Don't change the ground rules to suit the case, but be ruled by agreed upon laws, rules, and _"boundary markers."_

3. _Collect multiple true witnesses_ (vv. 15-20). Don't take one person's word for things, and make the penalties for breaking the ninth commandment (bearing _"false witness"_) so fearsome that the community will tremble (v. 20).

4. _Respond proportionately_ (v. 21). Rather than allowing spiraling escalation (vv. 6, 9) or discouraging honest, due process (vv. 19f), make sure the punishment fits the crime in a way that honors God, the perpetrator, and the victim.

There is never going to be a complete absence of conflict within the community of faith. But there are God-honoring ways of living together with accountability, justice, and due process. And the people of God are to honor boundaries and rules of fairness in life together, especially when emotions and tensions are high.

Exercise: _Of the four principles above, which speaks most pointedly to a conflict situation you are addressing? Meditate on how you will apply this particular biblical guideline today._

Deuteronomy 20

IDENTITY PRECEDES BATTLE

"When you go out to war against your enemies, and see horses and chariots, an army larger than your own, you shall not be afraid of them; for the Lord your God is with you, who brought you up from the land of Egypt." **– Deuteronomy 20:1**

You may have noticed that there is conflict from time to time in the Middle East today. Well, this is not a new thing. So Israel, like the other nations of that region, needed its stipulations regarding holy

Praying New Beginnings

war. Included are instructions about conscription (vv. 5-9), terms of peace, surrender or siege (vv. 10-13), and rules about spoils of war (vv. 14-18). There is also an interesting postscript about stewardship of the earth beyond the common scorched-earth policies of the day (vv. 19f).

The chapter, however, was most likely written many decades after settlement, and so exists for spiritual and theological reasons more than military purposes. God is to be thought of as the divine warrior who will *"go with you, to fight for you against your enemies"* (v. 4). In fact, the first issue (and most important) Deuteronomy 20 addresses is the spiritual condition of the people of God on the front end of battle. Israel is not to be racked with fear – *"do not lose heart, or be afraid, or panic, or be in dread of them"* (v. 3) based on the assets of the enemy. The people of God are not to be defined by the number of *"horses and chariots"* of *"an army larger than your own."* Rather, they are to remember who they are as people delivered from Egypt, and for whom the Lord will continue to fight.

Our identity is not determined by our enemy. We are not who we are because our opponent is bigger (or smaller) than us. Our sense of self is determined beyond the battle by who God is, and what the Lord has always done and will always do for us. Do not be swayed by the emotional ups and downs of anticipated victory or defeat. Remember that your identify precedes your battle!

Exercise: *In a current or pending conflict, how might I remember that my status of belonging to God is to govern my emotional state, and not the reverse? Ask God to help you remember who you are and who God is, and to let this - and not the enemy or the battle - determine your state of being.*

John P. Chandler 327

THE BIG POINT*

* OF THE FINE PRINT:

MURDER

"Absolve, O Lord, your people Israel, whom you redeemed; do not let the guilt of innocent blood remain in the midst of your people Israel." – Deuteronomy 21:8

Deuteronomy 21-25 is "case law" commentary on the second half of the Ten Commandments:

- 6th commandment (murder): Deuteronomy 19:1-22:8

- 7th (adultery): 22:9-23:18

- 8th (stealing): 23:19-24:7

- 9th (bearing false witness): 24:8-25:4

- 10th (coveting): 25:5-16.

Certainly some of the "fine print" is tribal and, as case law, is no longer applicable in our culture – for instance, commentary on slavery and polygamy in vv. 10-17. It is not dismissive of the power of Scripture to understand that we would today deal with a *"stubborn and rebellious son"* (v. 18) today by means other than stoning (v. 21)! What is important is to grasp <u>the big point of the fine print</u> in Scriptures such as these. That is a continual work taken up within the Bible itself, and work that Jesus himself does in the Sermon on the Mount. Just as in Deuteronomy, Jesus in Matthew 5 six times offers commentary on these same Commandments: *"You have heard that it was said ... but I say to you"* (Matthew 5:21f, 27f, 31f, 33f, 38f, 43f).

The big point of the fine print on Deuteronomy 21 instructions against murder is that bloodguilt leads to the pollution of the land, which leads to curse. The ancient Israelites had their ways of dealing with absolution (involving a *"heifer,"* v. 6), and we have ours. But in every culture, the people of God must deal with the sixth commandment decisively – whether murder in our land or murder in our hearts.

Exercise: *Just as Paul instructs us to follow not the "letter" but the "spirit" of the law (2 Corinthians 3:6), how can I look today at the fine print of something required of me, and neither*

a). get trapped in a literal and legalistic stranglehold, nor

b). dismiss the intent of the "fine print" of this Scripture for my life?

Today, specifically, how do I need to address "murder" around or within me, and pray for absolution?

John P. Chandler

THE BIG POINT*

*# OF THE FINE PRINT :

"Because the Lord your God travels along with your camp, to save you and hand over your enemies to you, therefore your camp must be holy, so that he may not see anything indecent among your and turn away from you."
– Deuteronomy 23:14

In the commentary on the second half of the Ten Commandments, it is easy to miss the forest for the trees. While there are mighty some strange verses in Deuteronomy 21-25, three important themes dominate:

1. The purity of land and people;

2. The sanctity of marriage and family relations; and

3. The importance of protecting and caring for others, especially the weak, vulnerable, and outsider.

Purity is not only matter of ritual cleanness, but of the moral and social order. It is a reflection of natural law and the created order. As Martin Luther commented on this passage, when all things *"are done decently and in order"* (1 Corinthians 14:40), God's gifts of simplicity and unity shine.

This is certainly true in the realm of sexuality. We no longer require *"evidence of the young woman's virginity to the elder of the city"* (22:15), for instance. But the big point of the fine print in the Deuteronomy 22-23 case law commentary on adultery is that purity and decency are connected with God being present among us.

When adultery runs rampant (22:22ff), when young women are abused sexually (22:25ff), when prostitution reigns (23:17f), it is safe to say that such indecency stands far from the holiness of God. If you want God in your camp, you do not violate the letter or the spirit of the commandment about adultery.

Exercise: *Take a fearless, searching moral inventory of your sexuality today. Is there anything that needs to be brought before the Lord for cleansing? If so, pray for God to cleanse you, and ask God to help you to live with decency in this expression of your life.*

John P. Chandler

THE BIG POINT *

*OF THE FINE PRINT:

"No one shall take a mill or an upper millstone in pledge, for that would be taking a life in pledge." – **Deuteronomy 24:6**

If Israel was going to learn to live well together, and to live well as a minority people within a new land, then they needed to learn how to treat one another fairly in matters of exchange. One of the clearest ways to do this was refusing to leverage the desperation of a neighbor for one's own financial gain.

Unlike loans to people from other nations, loans within Israel were a last resort, and usually due to financial desperation. Deuteronomy lists a number of different possible examples of desperation, including gleaning (23:24f), divorce (24:1-4), and kidnapping (24:7). The most poignant is the example of the "millstone." If a person is in such financial crisis that they have to loan out their very means of working their way out of those difficulties, then it is immoral to take advantage of that neighbor just because you can "buy low." It is "stealing" just as much as if you had robbed a bank. Commentator Patrick Miller summarizes: "The subordination of economic properties to the protection of basic needs (such as daily bread gained from the "millstone") is indeed deemed to be an explicit indicator of righteousness before God on the part of the members of the community."

It is one thing to be shrewd stewards and opportunistic to provide for yourself, family, and community. It is quite another to take advantage of the misfortune of a neighbor for your own gain. The big point of the fine print about stealing is that just because it is legal doesn't mean it is right.

Exercise: *Is there any way in which you are taking advantage of another's hardship to benefit financially? Look for one instance today where you can substitute generosity and sacrifice in place of frugality and shrewdness.*

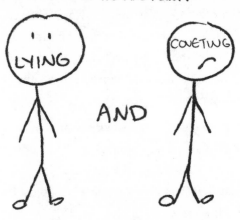

THE
BIG POINT *

*OF THE FINE PRINT:

LYING   AND   COVETING

"You shall have only a full and honest weight; you shall have only a full and honest measure, so that your days may be long in the land the Lord your God is giving you. For all who do such things, all who act dishonestly, are abhorrent to the Lord your God." – Deuteronomy 25:15-16

These two chapters list several instances where Israelites are acting in ways that are technically defensible as legal, but which rub against the intention of the Law. They may follow the *"letter"* but not the *"spirit"* of the Law (2 Corinthians 3:6). In other words, they take advantage of loopholes for their own advantage at the expense of someone else.

The climactic example of this is the practice of keeping *"in your bag two kinds of weights, large and small"* or *"two kinds of measures"* (25:13f). One customer – probably a peer or superior – gets one price per unit. Another – probably a vulnerable person such as a *"resident alien,"* *"orphan,"* or *"widow"* (24:17) – doesn't get the same good deal. The merchant uses a different weight because the poor person's back is against the wall and they are not in a place to demand fair treatment. The merchant gives a price according to a certain *"weight"* or *"measure"* – just not the same one as used for equals. In this sense, covetousness (a spirit of ravenous acquisitiveness) is fed by lying, or dishonesty. The tenth Commandment is broken by violating the ninth.

In our day, we don't still flog (25:1ff) or expect levirate marriage (25:5ff). But the principles here about lying because of coveting are the same. No matter the case, it is never going to be right among God's people for the "haves" to exploit the vulnerable "have-nots" – widow, orphan, and immigrant. To *"act dishonestly"* in matters of exchange is more than cheating a customer; it is nothing short of *"abhorrent to the Lord your God."*

Exercise: *Is there a current situation in which you may be tempted to use a double-standard for personal gain because you can leverage an advantage over the person with whom you are dealing? If so, what would it look like for you to act beyond what is "allowable" and instead respond with full integrity?*

John P. Chandler   335

Deuteronomy 26

WALK   KEEP   OBEY

"Today the Lord has obtained your agreement: to be his treasured people ... for him to set you high above all nations that he has made, in praise and in fame and in honor; and for you to be a people holy to the Lord your God, as he has promised." – Deuteronomy 26:18-19

There is a fundamental *"agreement"* between God and his *"treasured people."* God agrees *"to be your God."* In response, there are three descriptions of living up to our part of the *"agreement,"* and we are asked *"to observe them diligently with all your heart and with all your soul"* (v. 16):

1. To *"walk in his ways"* (v. 16) – this is an image of imitating and movement with God;

2. To *"keep his statutes"* and *"ordinances"* (v. 17; these are "case law" interpretations that ensure we preserve the spirit of God's intended *"ways"* for us in specific cases);

3. To *"obey him"* (or *"his commandments,"* v. 18).

It can be envisioned as a triangle which captures the movement of relational fidelity, honors the spirit of the Law in gray area cases, and does not skirt around direct instructions:

The outcome of such response is beautiful: God will "set you high above all nations that he has made, in praise and in fame and in honor; and for you to be a people holy to the Lord your God, as he has promised" (v. 19). When we walk, keep, and obey, our covenant response to God results in "praise, fame, honor" and especially holiness – a "promise" of God and beautiful witness to the world.

Exercise: Of the three ("walk, keep, obey,"), which are you most being called to enact next? Do you need to get moving, honor God's intentions in a fuzzy area, or be straight-up obedient in a matter?

"All the people shall say, "Amen!" – Deuteronomy 27:15-27**

Moses' sermon has continued unbroken since Deuteronomy 5, and will pick up again in the next chapter. But chapter 27 interrupts the monologue with a ceremony that dramatizes the covenant as a mutual agreement between God and the people. The monologue has to be a reaffirming dialogue if there is to be a covenant.

First, touchstones are set up to commemorate the significance of the ceremonial enactment of the covenant (vv. 2-9). Then, after a period of *"silence"* (v. 9), the twelve tribes participate in a call-and-response liturgy of twelve corresponding curses. Most of the curses have to do with rejecting dishonorable behavior done *"in secret"* (vv. 15, 24). If agreeing that each type of hidden behavior is bad, then *"All the people shall say, "Amen!"* This is repeated twelve times.

"Amen" means "truly," or "yes." It signifies agreement with what has been spoken. By saying *"Amen,"* the people ratify and validate what the leader says as their own belief as well. They thus affirm and adopt the covenant. This is why Moses says, *"This very day you have become the people of the Lord your God"* (v. 9). It's not simply a covenant because God gives the Law. It only becomes a covenant when the people say *"Amen!"* and embrace it for themselves.

A leader has not led simply because s/he has announced a vision. One becomes a leader at the point of having followers who have bought in enough to say, *"Amen!"* Once you have the partnership of *"Amen!"* then you can lead!

Exercise: *Whose "Amen!" do I need to hear today? Am I checking in with those I influence to monitor whether they are wholeheartedly embracing a shared vision, or am I assuming that just because I've said something, there is buy-in from everyone? Using the Deuteronomy 27 model, listen and call today for the "Amen!" of others rather than plowing ahead without waiting for a response.*

Deuteronomy 28

"The Lord will bring you back in ships to Egypt, by a route that I promised you would never see again; and there you shall offer yourselves for sale to your enemies as male female slaves, but there will be no buyer."
– Deuteronomy 28:68

This is Moses' second of three sermons in Deuteronomy (chapters 5-28 is the first, chapters 29-30 is the third). It consists of blessings (vv. 1-14) and curses (vv. 15-68). The noteworthy feature of this second sermon is that the curses are four times longer than

Praying New Beginnings

the blessings. Moses goes into great and gory detail about what will happen if the people make the unfortunate choice not to keep the covenant agreement into which they have entered with God.

Alarming warnings about the consequences of breaking off relationship with God are not isolated to Deuteronomy. Taking only a representative sample, Jeremiah 15 speaks death, sword, famine, captivity; Amos 4 adds hunger, drought, and pestilence; and Revelation 6 envisions these events in apocalyptic proportions. In Moses' sermon, hitting bottom meant a reversion to *"Egypt,"* the very symbol of slavery from which the Lord had delivered his people onto the threshold of the Promised Land. Beyond even siege and cannibalism, Moses in effect is saying, "Do you want to go back to something worse than *Egypt?"*

No doubt many prefer a genial, grandfatherly God who would never harm a fly. No doubt Moses would have preferred his farewell sermon to promise only blessings to his people. No doubt we would opt only for Jesus as mild enough for little children to come to him.

But the God of the covenant has very real expectations, and there are blistering consequences for blithely ignoring them. Moses did due diligence in telling Israel, "Consider yourselves warned." In like manner, every good leader will describe a reality where things can go very badly if we don't do well with our responsibilities.

Exercise: *Is there any instance in which you are shying away from naming the consequences of failing to follow through? Ask God to give you enough love for people to include appropriate warnings to them when called for.*

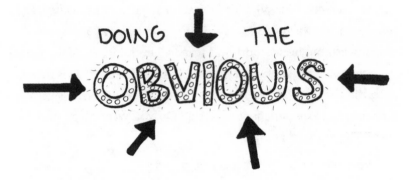

> *"The secret things belong to the Lord our God, but the revealed things belong to us and to our children forever, to observe all the words of this law."* – **Deuteronomy 29:29**

Moses' third and final sermon initiates a covenant renewal. He restates the covenant's demands and asks the people to reaffirm their commitment to it. He even gives them a hall pass as to why they have *"to this day"* (six time in chapter 29) only spottily obeyed – they hadn't yet been given *"a mind to understand or eyes to see, or ears to hear"* (v. 4).

Now, however, they have *"this book"* (v. 27), the Law. Now, they know fully and clearly what to do to maintain the relationship with God and are fully and clearly responsible. No need to dabble with other gods (vv. 17f); no need to wonder about divine mysteries (v. 24). All the people of God now need to do is to execute *"the revealed things that belong to us."* We are simply required to do what is clearly stated in the Law, to do the obvious.

Coach John Wooden frequently exhorted his players not to overthink and strategize the whole game, but to "do what's next," and execute the play right in front of them. Or as my tennis coach puts it, "Shots make points, points make games, games make matches, and matches determine the player you are." This is her way to help me focus on my next backhand rather than wonder about my career!

Not only does God graciously tell his people what it takes to be in relationship. God also gives us *"a mind to understand, eyes to see, and ears to hear."* God grants the ability to discern with clarity. Rather than inventing or synthesizing or speculating, God has offered clarity to us. Our role is to receive this gift and respond by doing the obvious things right in front of us.

Exercise: *What is the obvious thing God is asking you to do today? What is beyond doubt or speculation that God requires of you right now? Focus on executing <u>that</u> rather than seeking what God might reveal to you next.*

Deuteronomy 30

"Surely, this commandment that I am commanding you today is not too hard for you, nor is it too far away .... No, the word is very near to you; it is in your mouth and in your heart for you to observe." – Deuteronomy 30:11, 14

God's great invitation to us is that we do what is now, by grace, possible to do. Because God has *"gathered"* and *"scattered"* and will *"restore your fortunes and have compassion"* (v. 3), we now have the ability to make a choice about *"blessings and curses"* (v. 1). Obedience, once hopelessly out of reach, is now actually achievable because *"God will circumcise your heart"* (v. 6). Granted, it may take cutting of a painful sort, but it will make possible a *"prosperous and numerous"* life in the Promised Land.

This prophetic word, likely written while both writer and people were in Exile, presents the heart of the Old Testament: that life in the good and promised land of God is possible and doable. Paul later quotes these verses in Romans 10:9-13. He, too, proclaims the great good news: that because God has drawn near to us in person of Jesus Christ, the Good Life is *"near"* and *"in your heart for you to observe."* What was once impossible now becomes possible.

Leaders have to give people hope, to speak prophetic words of possibility. Hope is not a pipe dream. Hope is instead the empowerment that a better life in a better land through a better way is possible and doable. It is not a slam dunk, a done deal. But a better way is possible and doable when we make the right choices. Covenant relationship with God is not beyond reach!

Exercise: *How can I inspire others today with what is possible and doable? How can I challenge people to participate in a new and better way that does not seem far beyond their reach, but achievable by grace and effort?*

Deuteronomy 31

"The Lord said to Moses, "Your time to die is near; call Joshua and present yourselves in the tent of meeting, so that I may commission him." – Deuteronomy 31:14

The word "goodbye" derives from an old English contraction of the words, "God be with you." Of all that Moses did to lead the people of God – midwifing them from slavery to freedom, interceding to God on their behalf, brokering to them the Law that liberates – his final good work of leadership was to say "goodbye" well.

Praying New Beginnings

In a commissioning ceremony (vv. 14-23) enacting the handoff of the leadership mantle from Moses to Joshua, here is what a strong "goodbye" looks like:

- A reminder that task is more important than personality; *God* is the real leader!

- Calibration of assurance (vv. 8, 23) and challenge (v. 21) to the successor;

- Clarity about the divine source of authority for leading – it comes from God, not from personality (v. 3); and

- Final helpful instructions anticipating the next challenging stage of the journey (vv. 19ff).

Many a leader has done well while at the helm, only to stumble when passing the baton to the next leader. It can undo legacy, undermine gains, and place obstacles preventing the next leader's effectiveness. Often ego or insecurity is to blame. The onus on the current leader is to get his or her act together in time to work through those things, though. You haven't finished leading well until you have handed off well, giving your successor every opportunity to succeed. Often our final act of leadership is to say a good "goodbye."

Exercise: *How do I need to prepare for saying a strong "goodbye" and handing off well to the leader(s) who will follow behind me? List several goals for passing the baton and finishing your leg of the race well.*

Deuteronomy 32

MUSIC FOR THE MOVEMENT

*"Now therefore write this song, and teach it to the Israelites;
put it in their mouths, in order that this song may be a
witness for me against the Israelites ....And when many
terrible troubles come upon them, this song will confront
them as a witness, because it will not be lost from the
mouths of their descendants." –* **Deuteronomy 31:19, 21**

As Moses passes the mantle of leadership onto Joshua, he gives his final counsel, both to encourage and challenge his successor. In a commissioning ceremony (31:14-23), Moses instructs Joshua to write the song captured in Deuteronomy 32. Poetry and music can be a time bomb, and this song will be a prophetic confrontation that reminds the inevitably straying people how to correct back to the good way of God's Law.

Praying New Beginnings

The song itself recites both God's salvation (vv. 7-14) and Israel's rebelliousness (vv. 15-18). It is full of colorful language and artful imagery. The steadfast *"faithful God"* stands in bold relief to *"his degenerate children"* (vv. 4f). There is neither shrinking back from the challenge of corruption (vv. 28-33) nor hope for God's ability to vindicate in the face of it (vv. 34-43).

Furthermore, the song is *"no trifling matter for you, but rather your very life"* (v. 47). The music is not an optional frill but essential for future success. At the heart of the song are a series of images of God, who is like a:

- steady *"Rock"* (vv. 3, 15);
- a rescuing *"eagle"* (v. 11);
- nurturing mother (v. 19); and
- vindicating warrior (vv. 37ff).

Each of these images has the ability to land in the imagination of Israel and do its good work in its season.

Mike Breen says, "Every movement has its music," and Moses commissions this song to help the movement go forward. Leaders today would be wise to do the same. Just as a national anthem can galvanize a country, so also the right music, celebrating and challenging, can do what mere prose can never do to help a cause go forward.

Exercise: *What song captures the heart of where you are trying to accomplish with someone? If you don't have a song for your particular situation, ponder and pray until you do. Use the phrases and images of this song (for yourself and with those whom you lead) to call you through challenge and into faithful forward movement.*

"This is the blessing with which Moses, the man of God, blessed the Israelites before his death." – **Deuteronomy 33:1**

Like Jacob and Joseph before him (Genesis 27 and 48) and Joshua who would follow him (Joshua 23), Moses offers a deathbed blessing to the Israelite tribes. Plenty of scholarly ink has been spilled over omitted tribes (Simeon), demoted tribes (Reuben, v. 6), and transformed tribes (Levi, from warriors to priests, vv. 8-11).

However, it is important not to miss the main point of this climactic act from one who led Israel in unparalleled ways. Moses has warned the people, threatened and cajoled them, pleaded with them not to go astray. But when it comes time for his final words, Moses does none of these things. The time for all that has passed. It is now time for him to bless. And he does so in ways that are personal to each tribe, alternately remembering and hoping.

North Americans today typically fear a lingering death. But for most humans in history, the great tragedies were sudden deaths, when one did not have an opportunity to prepare to die. Part of preparing for death is to offer one's final blessings onto those around you. People who die well know how and whom they are going to bless. They do all in their power not to leave this earth without having done so.

Leaders with foresight give great thought to how and whom they will bless. They choose their words carefully and speak them personally. Few know the hour of their death, but most, with some intentionality, can prepare to bless. It is a powerful way to finish your race, and powerful help to someone else's race.

Exercise: *Who are the people whom you need to bless before you die? How do you plan to do so? Pick one of these people, and write out the words of blessing you want them to receive. Then ask God for guidance about when and how you will give them these words.*

John P. Chandler 351

WHAT MAKES FOR GREAT
SPIRITUAL LEADERSHIP?

*"Never since has there arisen a prophet in Israel like Moses,
whom the Lord knew face to face."* – **Deuteronomy 34:10**

What made Moses the giant of spiritual leadership in the history of Israel? Is it because of his prophetic work to speak truth to power (18:15-22)? Or because of his character as a humble, meek man (Numbers 12:3)? Was it because he overcame his deadly temper and interceded for the people when he had rather wiped them out? Or because he passed the baton of leadership successfully to Joshua before he died?

The final words of Deuteronomy — and of the Law — indicate that Moses' greatness was ultimately due to the fact that he was a person *"whom the Lord knew face to face."* Because of this intimacy with God, Moses was *"unequalled for all the signs and wonders that the Lord sent him to perform"* (v. 11) as well as *"mighty deeds"* and *"displays of power"* (v. 12).

It is a commentary that the final test of our ability to lead or influence others is based out of our primary relationship with God. To the extent that we have intimacy with God, we have the ability to lead others. It is truly, at the end of the day, not what you know, but Who you know. If you know God well, you will always be able to lead others well.

Exercise: *As you come to the close of this book, take stock of your intimacy with God right now. Is your relationship fading, stagnant, or growing? Assessing where you are, list a few key steps you need to take to get on the right relational path.*

Acknowledgements

Time and space are the media through which God creates, and through which we create. I would like to thank the dear people who have given gifts of time and space for writing this book. The beloved community they offer to me is a sign of the in-breaking Kingdom of God!

It is a joy to be enfolded within the world Baptist family, and John Upton symbolizes to me everything I love about my tribe: a global and Kingdom perspective, highly relational, and likeable, effective leadership. He is not only President of the Baptist World Alliance and Executive Director for Virginia Baptists, but the best boss I have ever had or seen! Thanks to John and to all of my friends and colleagues in the Baptist General Association of Virginia for the blessing and encouragement to work on this project. A shout-out to all in the "Uptick" tribe who are "winning the first battle of the day" and "working from rest." Thanks to David Bailey for creative and concrete conversation. Special thanks to dear friends and strategic collaborators Jim Baucom and Laura McDaniel – your vision, laughter, and partnership mean the world to me. Thanks to Laura and also Nathan White for turning this into a killer app!

Thanks to friends and mentors Alan Hirsch and Mike Breen – for personal encouragement and for teaching a new language: *oikos*, invitation/challenge, huddles, and LifeShapes. Thanks to my awesome community of faith, All Souls Charlottesville, especially to Jessica Luttrull for using God's gift of your art. Thanks to my friend and coach, Dan Elash, for years of helping me to clarify the Lord's calling on my life.

Finally, thanks to my sons, Preston and Roland, not only for Spanish inspiration, but for becoming great young spiritual leaders. And saving the best for last, thanks to the love of my life, Mary, for the idea to start this work, for the quiet time and space every morning to help me practice what I preach, and for the example of how to listen and respond to God with a generous heart.

"I thank my God every time I remember you, constantly praying with joy in every one of my prayers for all of you, because of your sharing in the gospel from the first day until now. I am confident of this, that the one who began a good work among you will bring it to completion by the day of Jesus Christ." – Philippians 1:3-6

Selected Bibliography

All Scripture quotes are from the New Revised Standard Version.

Note: In some instances, I have included a quote or idea from someone by name without citing a specific source. When no source is cited, this indicates one of several possible situations: that

1. *the quote or idea was cited within a commentary of another author listed below on that particular biblical passage, or*

2. *I heard it from them first hand in a personal conversation or sermon, or*

3. *I heard it attributed to them second hand orally in a lecture or conversation.*

I have done this in an order to reduce footnoting distractions or when I am uncertain of the original source. I hope readers will appreciate this intent. Authors, speakers, and historical citations are noted in the index.

— — — — — — —

Anderson, Bernhard. *Understanding the Old Testament,* Prentice-Hall, Inc., Englewood Cliffs, NJ, 1957.

Balentine, Samuel E. *Leviticus,* Interpretation: A Bible Commentary for Teaching and Preaching, John Knox Press, Atlanta, GA, 2002.

Blackaby, Henry, and Claude V. King. *Experiencing God: Knowing and Doing the Will of God, Revised and Expanded Edition,* B & H Publishing Group, Nashville, TN, 2008.

Breen, Mike. *Covenant and Kingdom,* 3D Ministries, Pawleys Island, SC, 2011.

____ and Steve Cockram. *Building a Discipling Culture*, 3D Ministries, Pawleys Island, SC, 2009.

Brueggemann, Walter. *Genesis,* Interpretation: A Bible Commentary for Teaching and Preaching, John Knox Press, Atlanta, GA, 1982.

_____. *The Collected Sermons of Walter Brueggemann,* Westminster John Knox Press, Louisville, KY, 2011.

_____. *Theology of the Old Testament: Testimony, Dispute, Advocacy,* Fortress Press, Philadelphia, PA, 1997.

Childs, Brevard S. *Exodus: A Critical, Theological Commentary,* The Westminster Press, Philadelphia, PA, 1974.

_____. *Introduction to the Old Testament as Scripture,* Fortress Press, Philadelphia, PA, 1979.

Collins, Jim, with Morten T. Hansen. *Great by Choice: Uncertainty, Chaos, and Luck – Why Some Thrive Despite Them All,* HarperCollins, New York, NY, 2011.

Foster, Richard J, Dallas Willard, and Walter Brueggemann. *The Life with God Bible NRSV,* Renovaré, Harper One, New York, NY, 2009.

Fretheim, Terence. *Exodus,* Interpretation: A Bible Commentary for Teaching and Preaching, John Knox Press, Atlanta, GA, 1991.

Gowan, Donald. *Genesis 1-11: From Eden to Babel,* International Theological Commentary, Wm. B. Eerdmans Publishing Company, Grand Rapids, MI, 1988.

Gregory of Nyssa. *The Life of Moses,* HarperCollins Spiritual Classics, Harper Collins, New York, NY, 2006.

Janzen, J. Gerald. *Genesis 12-50: Abraham and All the Families of the Earth,* International Theological Commentary, Wm. B. Eerdmans Publishing Company, Grand Rapids, MI, 1993.

Miller, Patrick. *Deuteronomy,* Interpretation: A Bible Commentary for Teaching and Preaching, John Knox Press, Atlanta, GA, 1990.

Niebuhr, Reinhold. *Moral Man and Immoral Society,* Scribner, New York, NY, 1960.

Olson, Dennis T. *Numbers,* Interpretation: A Bible Commentary for Teaching and Preaching, John Knox Press, Atlanta, GA, 1996.

Sakenfeld, Katharine Doob. *Numbers: Journeying with God,* International Theological Commentary, Wm. B. Eerdmans Publishing Company, Grand Rapids, MI, 1995.

Turner, Victor. *The Forest of Symbols: Aspects of Ndembu Ritual,* Cornell University Press, Ithaca, NY, 1970.

von Rad, Gerhard. *Deuteronomy,* The Old Testament Library, The Westminster Press, Philadelphia, PA, 1966.

_____. *Old Testament Theology: Volume 1: The Theology of Israel's Historical Traditions,* Harper & Row Publishers, New York, 1962.

_____. *Old Testament Theology: Volume 2: The Theology of Israel's Prophetic Traditions,* Harper & Row Publishers, New York, 1965.

Table of Scripture Chapters

(169 reflections overall)

Genesis 1-34, 35-36 (as one devotion), **37-50** (49 devotions total)

Exodus 1-11/12, 12/13-26/27, 28-36, 37/38/39, 40 (36 total)

Leviticus: 1, 2-3, 4-6, 6-7, 8-9, 10, 11-15, 16, 17, 18, 19, 20, 21-22, 23-27 (18 total)

Numbers: 1-2, 3/4, 5-25/26, 27, 28/29, 30-33, 34/35, 36 (33 total)

Deuteronomy: 1-21, 22/23, 23/24, 24/25, 26-34 (33 total)

Index

Get the free "Praying the Old Testament" app!

Go to www.SpenceNetwork.org/Praying on your Safari site.